The Qualities of an Ultimately Feminine Woman

By
Sandra K Schindler

To the women at *Ultimate Femininity* who have encouraged me to continue and supported me through the ups and downs in life. To Fairman, who has believed in me and convinced me to keep going and given me all the love I needed to believe in wonderful possibilities once again. I could only write this book because of him.

Contents

1
She is Feminine

Did you play house as a little girl? Did you ever play model show or dress up? Did you have tea parties with your little Teddie bears and dolls? Some of you may not have, but you may have had some distant yearnings to do so.

I remember going to a little friend's home to play and she had a pretend stove and sink and yes, even an ironing board! She had a crib for her dolls and a doll high chair, too. I loved playing house there. We would play house for hours, tenderly cooking, cleaning and caring for our babies. There was no hurry or rush to get things done. We enjoyed every second of our make-believe home.

Another friend had a huge trunk of dress-up clothes. We played with silky scarves and hats and gloves and frocks that came down so low we had to tie another scarf around our middles to hold them up. We wobbled about in high heels much too large and served each other tea and cookies and pretty little angel cakes. Sometimes I brought over my make-up and finger polish kit so that we would look especially beautiful.

Wonderful hours of enjoyable make-believe turned into real life soon enough. As a young wife and mother, I got lost. I wanted the babies and the job and the prince charming but somehow I was not doing a good job of it. I missed my babies when I worked and when I was home, I was trying to chase the clock to get everything done. So, I quit and stayed home full time. At first it was lovely. I caught up with the household but then, I felt left behind. I kept wondering what was wrong with me as I fought off depression. I went visiting others to try to find out what was working for them. I wanted to feel alive, to seek what I was trying to find and to escape my home that was feeling more like a prison.

That just put me behind and made me feel all the more miserable. So, I started to read. I grabbed hold of anything I could get my hands on for home making, marriage, and motherhood. I started to form ideas of what I really needed. It was all inside of me right from the beginning. That love of taking care of a home, of being a loving mother, of dressing like a woman and of being social and especially of being a wife, beloved among all women and held high on a pedestal by a man that I loved.

It had always been there, really. I had played and practiced it as a little girl. I had to love what I was doing. I needed to learn to live for the moment and enjoy every second of my life. I had to choose to be happy and choose to excel in my choice of working at home full time, finding fulfillment in a job most were casting off as too menial.

I spent more time with my children. Really learning who they were and what they liked. We had long conversations in the mornings before school work, outside in nature as we worked side by side in the house and each night before bed as I talked to each child individually. I began to really revel in motherhood and others noticed the tie I had with my kids and wanted to know my secrets.

I spent more time on my home. I took whatever means I had available to me and made my home sparkle. Polishing wood, and glass and keeping touch up paint for continuously clean walls made a huge difference. I would take all that was a permanent fixture of the home and make it work. Once I had yellow green carpeting. It was so out of style that it was easy to find things that would match it from resale shops and by the time I was done, the living room looked very cozy and neat even though we didn't have much money to spend at the time. I remembered that my grandparents didn't have new all the time I was growing up and their home was cozy. I didn't have to have brand new things to do the same. I kept to routines in cleaning the house and saw it as a way to show my family I loved them with each cleaning task I completed. I made it a home, a place to come back to and refresh, a place to bring their friends.

About that time, I also started putting interest into our meals. I baked things to always have something to offer to refresh my family or to entertain guests. Candles and flowers were added to the table. We started to decorate for season changes. More friends came to visit. There was a feeling our home gave to others that welcomed them and made them feel comfort. I especially enjoyed my adult tea parties with friends.

I also began to dress differently. My home was my work but that didn't mean I had to dress in jeans or sweats. I found I liked things that made me feel more womanly. It was fun to wear a skirt and put aprons on my girls and me when we did our big cleaning or were cooking. We dressed nicely when we went "to market" or on errands and people noticed and complimented. I started collecting things that made me feel more connected to my gender like scarfs, jewelry, hats, aprons, make-up and perfume. The more I did dress-up, the happier I became with who I was. I let my hair grow long too and had fun with different styles.

During all this time of change, I read and learned and applied what I was learning. My marriage was happier because I found that I could encourage and support rather than take over his role and try to make mine more like his. The opposite became true. The more feminine I became, the more manly he became in reaction to me.

This was what I had been looking for. My life had come full circle. I have remembered the little girl I was and gone back to what she loved and needed. I got lost during the teenage responsibilities I had of working, chores, and trying to be liked by boys because I thought that the more I was like them, the more I would be liked. I am looking back as a grown woman and understanding what society and family did to stifle what was a good and wholesome yearning.

I noticed that the little girls I fostered over the years had those same desires. They loved the things that I had loved as a little girl. Our house opened up to pretend cook stoves and dress up and tea parties. One little girl always told people that she wanted to be a mom when she grew up. I was always truly amazed at the reactions people gave to that desire. They would suggest that there were other things that were somehow better. They told her that she could also be a doctor or lawyer. I wonder if they would have been so quick to encourage her to be a homemaker or mommy if she had said doctor or lawyer. Those things as full-time jobs are no longer considered professions. How sad is that?

Our culture does preference the male sex. That sounds very feministic doesn't it? Do we treat our girls gender as less than our boys? Yes. And, part of it is because of the feminist movement. Is it ok for a little girl to wear boy's clothes? Now ask yourself, is it ok for a boy to wear girl's clothes? Is it alright for a girl to be seen as a tomboy? If a boy is seen as being girl-like is it seen as positive or negative? Interesting.

It starts way back then. Isn't that little baby girl so cute in those little overhauls? Who would possibly say that about a little boy in a dress?

I have a rewrite of the Dick and Jane books. Baby Sally is wearing overhauls most of the time. In the UF classes, I have encouraged women to go back to their childhoods and revisit some of their original gender thinking. The importance of doing this is to recognize what it feels like to be a girl without the influences society places on the preference to let little boys be boys but little girls be boy-girls. How soon does this come into play? Who doesn't think it is cute when a little girl makes car sounds when playing with toy cars? On the other hand, how does a father react to his son playing with the dolls or the dishes?

Men are not afraid to put down little girls by saying that a boy runs, plays ball, fights or cries like a girl. That same sort of man would not see it as a put down if he were to tell a girl that she played like a boy.

This sentiment has gone largely unrecognized in our society. Boys are not to be like girls but girls can be like boys and IF they are like boys, they are better some how. This needs to stop with us. We can enjoy our gender and love being girls and then inculcate this into our children. It is a good and fine thing for a girl to wear girl clothes and a boy to wear boy things. We should put strong definitions into boy and girl things. We can teach that there is a big difference in the way girls and boys are and then celebrate the differences and still teach that we are all part of the human family and can love and cry and be who we are without guilt.

Define the differences in what the girls in your family do and how they appear and then define it for the boys, too. They will follow your example. Feminism has done some wonderful things for us by giving us the vote and allowing women to be paid for what they do in the workforce, but it has just gone too far. We heard echos of "She can do anything he can do better". Well, Ultimate Femininity is above that notion. We do things better without resorting to competition with him, without taking away his roles and appearances. We don't have to run better and faster if we can meet him at the finish line, looking beautiful and worth running for.

This thing about taking men's blue jeans and making them tight and accentuating curves is not necessary. We can let him wear his jeans while we look better in something soft, touchable and flowing. We don't have to open our own doors, kill our own snakes or take away his pride in being protective of us. Yes, we know that we can if the circumstances made it necessary, but if we do it and take something away from him, is it worth it? These things are not tangible. They are there but not easy to put a finger on. They are important though because they have affected several generations now. It is time to see them for what they are, and put them far away from us. There will always be women who feel that we are being made door mats by choosing to cheer our men on instead of taking the race for him, but understanding the differences makes us the wise ones.

Sometimes people think that if you believe that the man is the spiritual head of the family that makes the woman insignificant dirt beneath his feet. This is not what we are about. The Grand Creator had two parts of a whole when he created man and woman. He knew that they both were being given free will and choice and preferences so He wisely supplied them with the tools to lead and to follow. He gave man some more physical strength and size. He made woman softer and more in tune with her emotions. This way the man could lead through the jungle paths but the woman could sense that there was a snake about to bite him and warn him in time, so to speak.

God knew that two captains on a ship would never work out. Both would confuse the crew (family) with different commands and perhaps chaos would ensue because of the competitive directing. So, what He did was the only logical decision. Make one slightly more able to take command. Make the other slightly more able to discern what the command meant but still be able to take over command if the captain was missing. What a miracle!

Ok, then what happened? People are imperfect. Men sometimes are not raised to know how to lead. But, mostly, something happened with women. Their mothers, society, school started to teach them that men were better and women needed to get better than men. Say what? How could this all get so confused? Well, the truth is that some men had taken advantage of the situation over the centuries. They got a little pushy with their wives and started taking things away and got all the worse as women fought against tyranny. These men weren't going to be pushed about. If you look into the far past, during the times of the scriptures, wives were owners of property and had respect in the world of men. Later this was not so true.

So where does this leave us in the time frame of the world? We are women of, and daughters of women of, the feminist age. It had some good but it is far removed from us. I personally believe that women are the best sex. Of course I believe that or else I would want to be a man or I would want to have what men have. Being fascinating, I let men think that they are better. Just teasing here, but really, I have no desire to fight for rights. Why should I? I went in quietly dressed in lace and silk and took my rights when I learned these things. And the men loved it! They swarmed at my feet at the foot of my pedestal. You all know what I am talking about don't you? What need do I have to fight anything? I am much too special to waste my time in it. I am far above it all. There is nothing that any man in this world has that I want or that he can take away from me. Think about this.

So are we to think that greater physical strength or power equals the best gender? I have seen women endure pain that would leave men screaming. I have seen women endure sadness that would make men run away. I have seen women defend a child, animal or someone else unjustly, unfairly wronged with a fury and strength that left all in the vicinity, man or woman, tremble in fear. My own example of finding the strength to carry on in spite of enduring one of the worse possible sights one can imagine makes me know the truth of these things.

No, this is not the way to decide who is better. Because men have that strength and use it to defend and care for those he loves without hesitation and for that I am grateful.

Could it be the money issue that tends to bring so much upset to marriages today? Does Ultimate Femininity teach that men are better and smarter so that only they can handle money? No. When a woman trusts a man she gives him her faith and belief that she trusts him to feed, clothe and protect herself and the children they have. She is saying that even though she is totally capable should the day come that she is without him, that she can hand over her life to him with trust. It is less about money and more about allowing him to slay the dragons in a world sadly lacking in dragons. If she really wants a knight in shining armor, a real man who is not afraid to be a man and is able to make decisions, he has to have a woman who is willing to allow him to lead. She chooses to do so.

You see, we don't have men who stomp all over us. We have men who we choose to lead us. We make an adult feminine choice to let that man be a man and to support him fully. The women who have taken a UF class understand that we let go of fights for rights and equal treatment. We know we have better treatment and we deserve it. We choose to hand over the dragons and let him slay them. We let him lead us through the jungle of life knowing that we can trust our senses about the snakes up ahead and that he can trust our abilities too.

I am not saying that both can't be done. If a woman needs to help support her husband and bring in financial help that is a wonderful thing for her to do for a time as long as she keeps the heart in her home. Even better if she can manage it from home. I really believe that a woman should have her own income, even if it is small so that she doesn't have to ask or beg for money. I will say more about this in the next chapter.

I was born female. I was not born feminine. I was the oldest of five children, the last two born after I was in my teens. I was my dad's best buddy until my brother was born. I became very hurt and jealous as a child over my brothers appearance into the world. It was obvious to me that he had usurped me in many ways especially in the bond with my dad. Looking back, I understand the sibling rivalry thing and can see it for what it was. At the time, I believed it was better to be a boy. I got better at being a boy at every opportunity. I climbed trees, I played with trucks and ignored my dolls. When I discovered boys, I learned about the things they liked. I worked on cars, raced motorcycles and went to trade school in a male profession. I married a transmission rebuilder at age 18 because it was a way to get out of the house. It seemed that my mother and I were constantly at odds. There were reasons for that animosity but I did not understand or know why back then.

Around me in the world, women were burning their bras and demanding equal pay. They were yelling out that they could do everything a man could do and do it better. Commercials shouted out in song that she could"bring home the bacon, and fry it up in a pan and never ever let him forget he was a man". That was very confusing to me. She should work and bring in money, cook and clean and be a sex kitten too? How could all that be accomplished?

As I said, my early years as a wife and mother were not good. Something was not working. My husband and I were not as close. I was actually jealous that he could go to work and leave me in a world at home that I did not understand and was not comfortable with. The world of "Father Knows Best" and the "Cleavers" was over and made fun of. The "Brady's" had a maid and were on their way out to be replaced with two working parent families like the "Huxtables". Those shows never explained who stayed home with the babies…oh no one did, they must have taken them to daycare! But no one could explain to me how to drop off this little one that I was so in love with to leave it with strangers all day. I never expected to feel that way. I didn't expect my marriage to be distant and I didn't expect to feel so depressed. I did everything I could to fix my husband and watched soap operas becoming more miserable day by day because my husband did not treat me the way the men on those shows treated their women.

As I stated, I started researching to find out what was missing, those things that I never understood. I read scripture. I read every marriage book I could get my hands on and finally I found "Fascinating Womanhood" and a book called "Total Woman". These books taught me that I would find my strength in being a woman. This was difficult for me to understand because I believe in my heart that it was bad that I had been so unfortunate as to be born of the "weaker sex". I read and researched some more. I learned more about submission and finally came to the conclusion that it was actually a responsible position of great strength and so was being a woman.

I began to embrace my femininity. Each and everything that made me feel more feminine was sought and loved. I learned that I love roses and the scent and it makes me feel happy. I learned that I love old-fashioned things like antiques and aprons and fans and scarves and pins. So be it! I was teased about accepting my inner female loves and it was hard. I had to really believe that I was entitled to love the things I did and stop being ashamed about it. Little by little, I gained strength in myself and in my being born woman. Then amazing things started to happen.

People began to respect me more, both male and female. They started seeking me out, wanted to have my company. I was self-assured, confident and interested in the happiness of others. I had a plan and was heading in a direction and my relationship with my husband blossomed. I was treated lovingly and with respect. No longer did I feel I had to be running the show. I quit running my husband too, and just made him responsible for his decisions. In learning how to let others be who they were, I got stronger and stronger. I learned deep secrets from the scriptures, that things were not really in my hands anyway so why be anxious. I learned that if I supported and chose to let my husband lead, then the blessings were abundant and I had much more power, respect and authority in areas than ever before. That the term "weaker sex" took on a new meaning. I began to see the genders more as two glasses, one a delicate, long stemmed wine glass and the other a stein type mug. Both were important, both could be put to good use but neither was better than the other. They just had different jobs. A feminine woman is not a weakling. She is courageous and strong. She is highly sought after and loved.

We need to re-learn acceptance of our feminine sides. Some of us may actually go far from center with it because we have learned to ignore the negative comments and finally achieved a comfort in our gender. It is ok to be a girl, even more, it is ok to enjoy being a girl.

Femininity is no longer considered a quality or even a gender role, it is considered a weakness. The sad truth is that we have nearly lost a gender in the goal for sameness of the sexes. Equality has come to mean that women should be equal to men but men are never equal to women. How can it really be equality if it is slanted in favor of one gender with the other gender lost, perhaps the feminine qualities gone?

The secrets of our femininity had almost been lost as well. UF is re-introducing them to generations who know something is missing to them. Being UF women means being among the strongest women in the world. UF women know men better than any others could. We have special understandings of how men think and feel and most likely will react under various circumstances. We don't compete with them, we enjoy the differences. We don't imitate men in our appearance, manner or routines. We carve out our own life based on what makes us comfortable as ultimately feminine women and we live in blessed harmony with the special man we have chosen. We revel in the changes he makes in response to our embracing our femininity. Our men are manly and happy. Our homes are happy and peaceful and our children are all the better for it.

2
She is Committed

The ultimately feminine woman has chosen the man she loves and committed to their relationship for life. She has also made a conscious decision to make a home that she is proud of in which to make him comfortable.

Women are caretakers. We are comfortable in that role. Men love to be taken care of to an extent. Some men who have been on their own for a while will say that they are self-sufficient and don't need to be waited on. It is true that he could carry on without a woman in the house should that need arise just as a woman can carry on without a man.

Still the more he allows his wife to do towards his comfort the more she will love him. The more she does towards his comfort, the more he will adore and appreciate her. No man wants a woman to feed him begrudgingly. How would he feel if she threw a potpie from the freezer in front of him? So she was too busy to cook that day? An UF woman is prepared for those times. How does he feel when he hears her complain that he is out of clean underware…again! What if he just yearns for a gentle neck and back rub after an especially difficult day at work? Does she do it half-heartedly or try to get it over with quickly or allow something to distract her? He would feel badly for having asked in the first place.

Some have suggested that we could spoil our men. This tender care and love is something he needs as much as he needs the air he breathes. He needs to know that she puts him first and that she is happy to make him comfortable and sees to his needs. He needs to know that she appreciates him and the work he does for the family and that his return home is a celebration. He needs to feel that she loves doing these little things for him and this makes him feel secure in the knowledge that he has a wife so willing to love him this way.

The following is a piece written back in the '50's. Many sources attributed it to Mrs. Helen Andelin, writer of "Fascinating Womanhood". She didn't actually write it. It was from an old home economics book but she does endorse the principle and so do I. Someone might have sent this to you as a joke. I have had it sent to my email a time or two when relatives or old friends didn't know that I owned a community that believes the old-fashioned values of male/female relationships are valid. These friends thought it was a hilarious out-dated idea that I would get a laugh out of. I didn't, I took notes!

The "Fascinating Womanhood" way to welcome a man when he comes home from work.

Get your work done: Plan your tasks with an eye on the clock. Finish or interrupt them an hour before he is expected. Your anguished cry, "Are you home already?" is not exactly a warm welcome.

Have dinner ready: Plan ahead, even the night before to have a delicious meal on time. This is a way of letting him know that you have been thinking about him and are concerned about his needs. Most men are hungry when they come home and the prospects of a good meal are part of the warm welcome needed.

Prepare yourself: Take 15 minutes to rest so you will be refreshed when he arrives. This will also make you happy to see him instead of too tired to care. Turn off the worry and be glad to be alive and grateful for the man who is going to walk in. When you arise, take care of your appearance. Touch up your makeup, put a ribbon in your hair and be fresh looking. He has just been with a lot of work-weary people. Be a little gay and a little more interesting. His boring day may need a lift.

Clear away the clutter: Make one last trip through the main part of the house just before your husband arrives, gathering up school books, toys, paper, etc. in a bucket or wastebasket and put them in the back bedroom for sorting later. Then run a dust cloth over the tables. Your husband will feel he has reached a haven of rest and order and it will give you a lift too. Having the house in order is another way of letting him know that you care and have planned for this home coming.

Prepare the children: Take just a few minutes to wash the children's hands and faces and comb their hair, and if necessary change their clothes. They are little treasures and he would like to see them look the part.

Minimize all noise: Especially give heed to this if your husband has to join rush hour traffic. At the time of his arrival eliminate noise of washer, dryer, dishwasher or vacuum. Try to encourage the children to be quiet at the time of their father's arrival. Let them be a little noisy beforehand to get it out of their system.

Be happy to see him: Greet him with a warm smile and act glad to see him. Tell him that it is good to have him home. This may make his day worthwhile. If there is any romance left in you, he needs it now.

Some don'ts: Don't greet him with problems and complaints. Solve the problems you can before he gets home and save those you must discuss with him until later in the evening. Also, don't complain if he is late for dinner. Count this as a minor problem when compared with what he might have gone through that day. Don't allow the children to rush at him with problems or requests. Allow them to briefly greet their father but save demands for later.

Make him comfortable: Have him lean back into a comfortable chair or suggest he lie down in the bedroom. Have a cool or warm drink ready for him. Arrange his pillow and offer to massage his neck and shoulders and take off his shoes. Don't insist on this however. Turn on music if it is one of his pleasures. Speak in a soft, soothing, pleasant voice. Allow him to relax-to unwind.

Listen to him: You may have a dozen things to tell him, but this moment of his arrival is not the time. Let him talk first, then he will be a more responsive listener later.

Make the evening his: Never complain if he does not take you out to dinner or to other places of entertainment. Instead, try to understand his world of strain and pressure, his need to be home and to relax. If he is cross or irritable, never fight back. Again, try to understand his world of strain.

The goal: Try to make your home a place of peace and order where your husband can renew himself in body and spirit. He will rather be with you than anyone else in the world and will spend whatever time he can possibly spare with you. Try living all of these rules for his homecoming and see what happens. This is the way to bring a man home to your side, not by pressure, persuasion or moral obligation.—author unknown

If this seems funny to you, change it around. Think about how you would feel after coming home from a very hard day of work to have this all done for you. Would you appreciate a little peace and quiet to buffer you from the world a bit? How about a nice cool drink? Would it be grand to smell good food smells and see the table set ready to receive you and the family?

What comes to mind is the comedy of the father who dresses as an older woman to care for his own children, "Mrs. Doubtfire". Remember the scene when the wife comes home to hear the words "Dinner is served, Madam" and there is a beautiful table set with candles. This is exactly something that each of us would appreciate. If we are homemakers, it is a great privilege to give this gift to our husbands. If our situation dictates that we must work away from home, can we hire this privilege or is there a way to do it at least a few times a week? Having a good, loving relationship is worth so much. If your heart is in your home, you will do all that you can to get this for yourself and the ones you love.

If you spoil your husband, you will love him all the more and he will know just how much you appreciate his going out into the world to work hard for his family. I know of a man who lost his wife and he told me how difficult it was to work now. He told me that when things would get tough on the job, he could look down at his wedding ring, touch it and remember that his wife loved and needed him. Knowing that she was at home waiting for him, made it all worthwhile. After she was gone, it was difficult for him to keep going.

I bet your husband feels the same way. A man will do without so many things for the love of a woman. Think about it. His income would be much greater without a wife and family. He could more often go where he wanted and do what he wanted without having to consider her feelings on the matter. Instead, he gets up in the morning and faces a working world and gives up his income for her. So, isn't this worth a celebration each night he comes home to you?

If you haven't been celebrating your husband's homecoming, try it and see if the results you get aren't much better in how YOU see things and how he reacts to you.

Ultimately Feminine women are not weaklings. We are strong women who have happened to go into a detailed study of the differences between the genders. We understand men like no other women on this earth. We don't dummy ourselves up to get along with men. There is a huge difference between stupidity and using tactful ways. Let me give you this illustration:

You and your dear husband are in the car looking for a parking spot. He is driving. You spy an open spot up ahead and say : "There's one! Park there!". He might , but it also might more appeal to his manly demeanor if you said instead: "I see a spot up there, honey. Do you want to use that one?" Sometimes, asking in question form is tactful and demanding statements aren't. If you don't see this point, substitute your husband for your boss instead.

UF does teach that the husband is the head of the house and the woman is it's heart. Having two captains on a ship will sink it. With all this said, we also view our stated submission to the captain of the ship as a choice that we make freely and certainly NOT something that enslaves us.

As for the fun made of greeting husbands at the door, I think that if you put yourself in there as being treated that way after a hard day of work, you can see that it is all based on kindness.

You aren't going to spoil him so that he is impossible to live with. This is something he needs as much as he needs the air he breathes. He needs to know that you put him first that you are happy to make him comfortable and care for his needs. He needs to know that you appreciate the work he does for the family and that his return home is a celebration. He needs to feel that you love doing these little things for him. It makes him feel secure that he has a wife so willing to love him.

Occasionally, a man will get used to all of this and forget himself and take his wife for granted. There are ways to handle that and I will get to that later in the chapter. For the most part, men need and want a woman who goes out of her way to make him happy and he will treasure her.

We are not robots or "Stepford Wives". The difference is that we are wise enough to know that this makes a difference in our relationship with our spouse. We aren't under obligation, or being forced, we have made a choice to make our marriage the best it can be and we know that if it is for our own needs, feeling even more love, that we go out of our way to bring happiness and comfort. It is a small thing that makes such a huge difference.

This does apply to our children as well. When you have 25 children come through your home, as I did when I was a foster parent, believe me there are going to be some children that are easier to love than others. I believe in the philosophy that if you take care of something more, you will love it more. So, I would make it a point to give special attention, personally, to the child that I was having trouble bonding with. Not for the child's sake, for my own. The more I bathed, read to, cuddled with this child, the easier it became for me to love her.

Have you ever found that you did not feel a bond with an individual, maybe didn't even like that person until you were put into a situation where you had to care for her? I remember a best friend I had, Gina. When we first met, we were at odds, it seemed like on almost everything. But one day, she needed me to help with a problem child. After working together to find some answers to this child's problems, we became quite close. I called to offer more assistance or to give support and it seemed the more that I went out of my way, the closer we became. I found probably one of the best friends of my life.

This ideal works. It makes a huge difference when you look at it logically. But the difference is going to be more in YOU than in those you comfort and support and tend to.

Were you told not to spoil your child? Not to pick him up when he cried, not to give him a blanket or stuffed animal because you would pay dearly later? I ignored this advice. I don't believe you can spoil a young baby because the only way they have to communicate is by crying and showing discomfort. Little ones need to know that they can depend on their mothers to be there for them. The sad outcome for little ones who did not have that is something called RAD, Reactive Attachment Disorder. I have had several children in my care with this diagnosis.

RAD happens when the bonding just didn't happen between a baby and his mother during the first few years of the child's life especially during the first year of life. This is when a baby needs are touch, eye contact, movement, smiles and nourishment. When the baby has a need, it is expressed through crying. Under the best circumstances, the mother recognizes and satisfies the need. This interaction happens thousands of times and the little one learns that the world is a safe place and can then mature to the ability to trust using this trust as a secure base from which the child can explore the world.

Sometimes things go wrong and this initial bonding just doesn't happen and the children never gain the ability to trust that the world is a safe place and that others will take good care of them. The children believe that they must be hyper-vigilant and see about their own safety. They put up a strong wall emotionally keeping others at a distance. They are afraid and they become extremely demanding, controlling and manipulative. They really feel that their life depends on their being in control of their world.

There are also some physical things that happen to these kids. They have very high stress hormones and this can change how they grow and definitely can affect the brain development. They can be without morals, aggressive, disruptive and antisocial. They have learned that the world is a scary place and you can't trust anyone. As you can imagine, it is very difficult to parent a child like this.

Fairman, my fiancé, was very good at giving his children this care and love. He raised both his daughter and son with a lot of hugging, kissing and warmth. This was especially important because he raised his son alone from the time of the boy's adolescence. I had a chat with this young man, now in his twenties, away at college. He shared with me how happy he was to have a girlfriend because the family had always been "huggers" and he had really missed that sort of contact while at college.

Now taking this extreme into another relationship, the marriage, where love and caring also take place, doesn't it stand to reason that touch and nurturing and care should be a part? Is it spoiling to do so? No! It is simply a way to build attachment, bonding and trust. A way to bond that is far beyond sexual touch.

I bet some of you are trying to accept what I am saying here but still feel those old familiar bristles. "I should be the one that is pampered. Why should I do anything special for him? He is a grown man and not some baby to be tended. I have my hands full enough. I work, too. I have to take care of kids all day and then BABY HIM?"

Stay with me here. UF teaches that the more deeply we care for someone or something, the closer we get to them. The bond is built stronger between mother and child as she bathes, feeds, changes him. Our Creator was so smart to make babies little and completely dependent, forcing a mother to care. The more she tends to that little one, the more she loves it. This same philosophy has turned up in our UF Home Ec Course. The more we care for our homes, the more we put into it, the more we love them. Those who home school have found that when they really get into their lessons, there is a better bond built with older children. The friends we tend to are the ones we are closer to. The flower gardens we give our hearts to, flourish and we love them all the more. Could it be any less with our spouse?

By pampering our husbands we build something special into the relationship but it is more for our own sakes that we "spoil" them. It changes us. It makes us love them all the more.

Yes, there may come a time when that baby needs to not take for granted that he will get everything he wants in life. Mom loves him enough to tell him "no" sometimes. And when it comes to men, yes, they can get to a point where they may try to take a UF woman for granted. Huge mistake! We are princesses! No one dares take us for granted because we will, out of kindness, of course, show them the error of their ways. But just think…it takes many months of gentle love and care and always being available for that bond to be made between mother and child. By the time the baby is mobile, reaching for electrical cords and crawling towards stairs, that bond has been built so strong that the baby knows that horrid word "no" is said by the love of his baby life and she will always be there for him. He can trust that she loves him and knows what is best for him even if he is heart broken that she won't give him that pretty cord in the wall socket to play with. With the other love bond, the marriage one, too many husbands do not have the confidence in that bond to know for sure. So pamper him, bond with him, give your all to him and let him know that he is number one in your life. If anyone suggests that you spoil your husband…thank them for the compliment!

Wow! What a man will do for the woman he loves. When he decides to marry, he gives up many things, his freedom mainly. He no longer can live only for himself. Now he must consider all his options carefully because he is responsible for two persons or more if there are children. Even in this modern world, men still feel that responsibility and it weighs heavily on their shoulders.

When he was single he could do as he wanted and spend his money in even foolish ways without fear of serious consequences. Often, he could stay out late and take chances that a family man would not consider. Whether his wife is bringing in an income or not, a responsible married man worries and cares strongly about the needs of his family first and foremost. Many work long hours to provide for loved ones.

Things can go bad the other way, too. If you consider taking him for granted, stop and consider how much further ahead he would be financially if he had not loved you enough to bring you into his home. How easy his life would be if he just had himself and no one else to worry about.

I am not suggesting that you bring nothing of worth to the pot. Of course you do and he knows it. He wants you and needs you and all he desires in return is your love and respect. He knows the quality of his life is much better because you are in it. But don't for a second take this all for granted. I know very well, how quickly it can be gone because one day I found myself as a widow. And there are many men who choose a life without ties and revel in it. They all wanted to date me. No ties, but sex would be good. And be aware that there are plenty of women out there who would love to have your man and do not appreciate boundary lines. It is only wise to understand these things.

What makes a man commit to a woman and give her his heart and soul and makes him want to share all that he has with her? An aching need to share his life with a woman who understands and appreciates him. A need to walk down life's path with a mate who will laugh and cry with him as they meet the adventures that the future brings. A woman who has a warm heart and feminine charms. She might not be the prettiest or the smartest or even have the best figure, but she loves him, admires and appreciates him and gives him all she has to give.

Do you show you support your husband in his career? Get up with him and send him off with hugs and kisses. Feed his stomach and his soul before he faces the world filled with people who don't know his good traits the way you do. He will deal with some tough situations during the day. Show him that you are with him by being conscious and supportive in the morning. One man complained to me that his wife made him stop kissing her good-bye in the morning. She was in bed and needed her sleep, was how she told him and he was crushed by this. Remember the man who would look down at his ring for the strength he needed throughout his long day.

Make him breakfast if he will let you. Pack his lunch, maybe add a little note if you know he has a special goal to reach that day. You might lay his clothes out and maybe help dry off his back when he gets out of the shower. I personally love to watch a man shave in the morning because it is such a manly thing to do. Kiss him and tell him to hurry home to you. Wave at the door as he pulls out. Be his number one fan. Be his support. You know there are lots of other women jealous of you and the man that adores you.

And remember that when he comes home to you, tired and beaten down, that he could have stopped off at his buddy's house or the local bar, to look for a kind word or appreciative glance. Give him a hero's welcome because he deserves it. He is the protector and provider and champion of the family. Let the children run and jump and shout that he is home. Slip into his arms and kiss him like you haven't seen him in a year and let him know that you are just so glad he came home to you!

Sometimes we come across a woman who complains bitterly about her husband. Sometimes, he is not really that bad a guy. The old saying that misery loves company is often true with women like this. They want to have people commiserate with their horrible life. They are yelling loudly: "Feel sorry for me, I am a wretched creature because I am married to a horrible man." Unfortunately, what is often heard is just the opposite. Others may hear: "She loves to complain and get pity." or "What is wrong with her? She picked him out didn't she?"

I remember as a young wife feeling so very sorry for myself because my husband worked a lot of hours and didn't treat me the way the sexy men on the soap operas treated their women. I found lots of things wrong with my husband and found listening ears. One older woman listened to my tale of woes and sighed. She said that when she sat at my wedding, she had such bright hopes that we would have a lovely happy love affair. She was just so heart broken that it was not to be.

She got me thinking. She got me searching and she got me studying. I put aside my soap operas in favor of books on marriage. This study helped me to understand that I already had everything! I had a man who adored me and showed it by working very hard. I had a real man who was passionate with me but not every single night. Just the fact that I had a husband when so many others are single was a gift from heaven.

I decided that very year that whatever would happen, I would choose to be happy and I would choose to have the very best marriage possible. That was the year I found out that it was all within my hands! It was very freeing.

Now, I am not saying that there aren't some real problems with some men. I have been through my share. If it became a situation where my children or I were in danger or perhaps others, including my husband, himself, I totally believe that a marriage should be saved by ending the danger. Let me explain. If a husband drives drunk and is an alcholic...for his sake, for the children's sake, I would ask him to live else where (or I would take the children and move out) while he gets himself together. For me, this would mean six months of sobriety, and a 12-step program and perhaps counseling. It would be a supreme act of kindness to offer him this opportunity to save the marriage. It would be an opportunity from a woman who cares deeply about her marriage and her husband, that she would take on the unfair duty of head of household for this time period. Now, I am not saying that everyone should do this if a husband has an occasional indiscretion and is not a danger to anyone. Nor would I ever make a decision for anyone else regarding a temporary separation. I am saying that a strong woman occasionally must make a decision about separation for the sake of saving the marriage.

If a man is unfaithful, there is nothing that anyone here would say against a temporary separation to allow him to get his head together with the hope that the marriage might be saved. On the other hand, if a woman felt she could never forgive him, it would be best to divorce.

Regardless of those difficult decisions, a woman of character never lets anyone know or see anything except a good face forward. A UF woman holds her head up because she is a princess. She chooses to be happy regardless of what stones are thrown into her path. The scriptures talk about us being a spectacle to the world. Angels watch as we walk our earthly travel and we either make them smile or we make them turn away. We all will be tested. We all will be sorely hurt but we all make choices to adapt to our life and be the best that we can be no matter what.

I understand that sometimes, it helps to pour out your soul to a safe friend. If you don't have someone in your life, find a mentor to act as an "older women". Mentors are offered at our website www.ultimatefemininity.com

So everyone, please understand that UF teaches always to look to your husband's better side and if you can't do that, please, please say nothing at all. It does you no good and it keeps you from moving forward to good results.

I ran a poll a while back and found that there were some very interesting results. The poll filled out by members of the UF community showed that the majority of our members are full-time homemakers. In a close second place are those who work full-time outside the home. A small few of the members have part –time jobs or work from home. After reading the results of the poll I did some research and found that there were 5 main reasons for a marriage to dissolve according to the American Academy of Matrimonial Lawyers. Here is the list:

Poor Communication
Financial Problems
Lack of Commitment to the Marriage
Dramatic Change in Priorities
Infidelity

That first one, poor communication, is something that we as UF women work very hard at. We know "manspeak" and try to understand the differences in how men see things and the way we do. A big part of the success of doing this is in accepting our husbands the way that they are and not making it our business to change them into who we think they should be. We respect our husbands so that when they make a request of us, we take it seriously and do our best to fulfill the request. We appreciate our men and are not afraid to tell them, even many times a day, that we admire them and the hard work they do for us. When our husbands talk, we listen without butting in. We might not always understand or agree but we appreciate and love the man enough to let him have his say.

We have a relationship built on a long time of trust and have no fear of expressing our needs and desires and yes, even our concerns. Speaking up is part of the responsibility of a first mate. Giving opinion when it is asked for is also a privilege. In turn, our husbands have come to trust our words and intuition.

The second problem marriages face is financial problems. In the past many women were homemakers and did not work outside the home. They were completely dependent financially on their husbands. Sometimes, this was not the best situation. Some women felt that they had to beg their husband for money for just about anything and it was degrading for them. I feel that this may have been part of the yearning that some women felt and for the number of women joining the workforce in the last few generations. Surely there is a way for a woman to have this feeling of being able to spend money on things she would like without having to ask for it. Two ways come to mind. One is that a firm budget can be set up with both husband and wife having discretionary funds. The other is that the wife earns some money of her own.

For the Christians reading this book, have a good look at the woman of Proverbs 31 who was very capable and of the many things listed in those scriptures about her, was her business sense and financial abilities. She bought land, started a business and made it very profitable. The key to this bringing happiness to the family is that she put her home interests first and did not compete with her husband in earning capability. He was a prominent man known in the gates of the city meaning that he was fairly wealthy. So why did she have to go long distances for the things she wanted to buy at a good price? Why did she have to work? She didn't.

The lesson to me is that we can make money without it becoming an issue of competing. Men want and need to be the top bread winner. If a woman can overtake him in that role or even if they keep seeking to do so, the marriage will suffer. Many have not taken into consideration the basic make-up of a man and his needs. There are varying circumstances of course. In my example, I received an inheritance after my husband's death and my way of handling it is to use my monies for household expenses or special things that I want after I remarry. Substantial funds might be used for investments or following the lead of the virtuous woman of Proverbs, purchase property.

Don't fall into the trap so many women have fallen into since women's liberation began it's battle, in striving to outdo the man you love. I know of a situation where the wife constantly was trying for the big bucks. Going to college, getting degrees after her children were born and then still not happy because she could not get the kind of money her husband did. She openly competed with him and he knew it. This marriage was doomed because she had no appreciation for the hard work he put into his career for her sake and the sake of the children. This is a main difference between the genders in careers. A woman will go into a career for her own needs. A man will go into his career to care well for those he loves. Of course, there are some exceptions but this is a basic for the most part. Don't set out to win, to better him, instead, always give him your support.

Some women go too far in the other direction. They spend up and beyond the family's budget, often using plastic to do so. I know of several ended marriages where the husband spent years repaying credit debt that his ex-wife had tallied up.

There needs to be a balance. Bring in money that you won't have to beg for but don't over spend it or make it a focus of your life. Learn how to invest it and make it grow. A great scenario is to create a home based business or service whenever possible. Home should be where our heart is. If we are working from home, we can keep attention on the important things that are necessary in running a home. Use some funds to help others secretly. Have an emergency fund set aside that will add to the security of the family. After David died, it was a while before the checks came in from life insurance. I still had a mortgage and now a funeral to pay plus the regular bills. We had been saving pennies in a plastic water jug and I sent my two sons to the bank with it. That $395.00 was a true blessing. Even saving pennies makes sense.

Some of you are in that situation of needing to work because it takes two incomes to survive. I wish I could change that. It is so unfair that our economy is set up this way now. But do, please, really look for the time that with careful planning you can be home again. It is so much better for the family if there is an at-home mom/wife.

One more thing, don't fret about having money in case the marriage doesn't work. Those of you who do that are dooming your marriage to fail. That brings us to the next point brought out by the lawyers, the lack of commitment to the marriage. These days, marriage is so easy to get out of. Close to half of all marriages end in divorce. The hard part of marriage is to stick with it. There are going to be good times and bad. Sometimes you might not feel like you love him any more but do yourself and your husband a favor and take the UF Marriage Enrichment course. Don't go see a lawyer. Learn how to rekindle that first love and how to add some spice to it. It is worth it!

The next problem facing marriages is facing a dramatic change in priorities. Often it is happening because a woman takes on a career. She is tired, and feels unappreciated. He doesn't understand and he feels unappreciated and no one is looking after anyone anymore. Home is no longer the woman's priority and she expects her husband to take on half the responsibilities. He isn't equipped and doesn't really know how and chaos ensues.

Sometimes, a child enters the pictures and changes the dynamics of the relationship. Some women focus on the child and the husband must take the back seat instead of being number one in her life, which is his rightful place. It is true that babies are helpless and their care must interrupt schedules. Husbands do understand this and don't want their child to be neglected but a happy relationship must be tended and if that is neglected all members suffer.

Some women change priorities in how they appear or in neglecting their health. Depressed women often will gain weight and their health will deteriorate. I believe this happened to me in my first marriage. We all put on weight as the years pass, but to ignore totally our human upkeep or to let our bodies to become unkempt makes us spiral in unhappiness. We speak about "filling our glass" in UF. That means that we don't have anything to pour out on the others in our life if we don't do things to make ourselves feel good and happy. On bad days, the first thing I have to do is bathe and get my hair and make-up done. Then I feel more equipped to face the world.

I know that a man can also be the cause of the change in priorities but this is a book written to women so I have you to work with. If any of these things apply to you, take the steps you need to take right away.

The last problem facing marriages today, is infidelity. As I said already, if you can forgive, do so. If you can't it is time to leave the marriage but there are so many possible reasons why a man might stray. As for the women out there, if you are considering this, it is just not worth it. You change one set of problems for another and often the new set is worse. Work on yourself, work on your marriage. Don't cover up problems, fix them!

Women new to UF classes often are amazed at what a difference is made in their relationship. They report feeling the way they used to feel when love was new. There are reasons for this.

We encourage women to really put their husbands wants, desires and needs first before their own. They are taught to really saturate him with love. To go out of their way to show him how much they need and appreciate him. Some say the definition of love is when you would rather your mate be happy than you. I think that is pretty close. UF women take responsibility for the celebrations and romance that happens in their home. I wanted to focus some on the romance aspect.

Think back to when your husband was courting you. What was it that first attracted him to you? What was it that you loved about him? His eyes? The way his hands gripped the steering wheel? His wonderful sense of humor? Do you remember how you felt? I can talk about this since I am in a new relationship and feeling all of those things. That feeling that envelopes your soul so much that you can feel it when you breathe. It puts butterflies in your tummy and his touch on your hand is electrifying. It is bittersweet. It is so wonderful but it can't last all the time or you would be swept away by it. And gee...nothing would get done!

But if you make him the king in your home, he will react to it. He will put you up higher than all creatures. He will all but worship you. And when the lights are low and life has been sweet, there is a good chance that all those feelings and emotions will play out for you once again...and again and again. You can make these things happen. You hold it in the palm of your hand. You can make your husband want you like he did when he first loved you.

If you are in a slump, get out some of those old love letters. Put on some romantic music. Plan a special dinner and an outing without the children. Plan a date night. Challenge him. Tell him you will meet him at such and such a place. Just make sure you are there! I sent my husband a note one day saying I would be ready and waiting for him at 1:30. I never thought he would leave work and just meant for it to be a tease. He came home!

UF women prepare themselves for intimacy every evening. They figure that if it happens, wonderful, and if not, this is only one night out of the rest of their lives and the privilege of sleeping next to this man is enough for them. Still they do prepare. I always liked to have a separate area for me to change. There should be some mystery. He doesn't need to know how much care you give to keeping smooth and stubble free. He doesn't need to watch you pluck or dye or paint.

There are some things that make a man's heart skip a beat. Watching his wife brush her hair is one that comes to mind. I wish I could buy a vanity table for all of you. Imagine softly brushing your hair watching him watch you in the mirror. Another romantic thing is to make the bed in the morning and spray a bit of your perfume on the sheets while he watches. Turn around and say "hurry home tonight, dear". He will get the hint.

Do you walk him out to the car in the morning? Try it. Walk him out and wave until he is out of sight. We have discussed celebrating his return but sending him off could be a ritual that gives him just what he needs to face the day. What??? am I hearing some whispers out there about your still being in bed? Not UF women. They get up with him to give him the support he needs. They don't let him face a single morning alone. They are a team and that is how UF members let him know it.

I also recommend that you spend some quality alone time. Send the kids off to grandmas. All parties will appreciate you more when the kids get home. This isn't the weekend that you remodel the bathroom. This isn't a weekend to spend in the kitchen. This is time to focus on each other. UF often talks about pampering ourselves...filling our glass. If you have done this, teach him how to be pampered. Men don't know how to do this for themselves. It doesn't seem masculine to them. So you can pamper him. Have a warm fluffy towel ready for him when he steps out of the shower. Use lotions and powders to relax and care for his skin. Men totally ignore their feet and most will appreciate your giving them the care they need.

Remember too, that textures can be soothing. A woman's clothing should be soft, silky, smooth maybe lacy. Men can't wear such things and it may be the only opportunity he gets to feel them. If you wear t-shirts and underwear to bed, he won't have the opportunity to appreciate silky things. The same goes with flowers and candles. Unless there is an outage, he isn't going to light candles. But that doesn't mean he won't appreciate them.

All of this is important to strengthen the bonds between the two of you. He isn't going to get a swelled head with all this attention. In my experience...I have found that men are more likely to be needing attention than getting too much. You will know when he needs to be wheeled back a bit. If he starts taking you for granted, expecting you to do these things or doesn't take your feelings into consideration. There are things that can be done when that happens. You see UF women are saucy! They have spirit and a zest for life! They don't mope if things aren't fair. They do something about it! And the more spirited and saucy the better.

There are 3 levels of being upset with a spouse.
1. The day to day irritations
2. A medium offence
3. A heart crushing pain that he caused you

Before you say a word, before you even begin to react, categorize the hurt. Is it a category 1, 2, or 3? Understand that in a long-time relationship, all three are going to occur. I want to take you through them step by step with what women do and what UF saucy, spirited wonderful women do.

A level one hurt. He forgot to take out the garbage, again.

A woman of the world will yell out how hard she works and all he has to do around the house is take out the garbage and he is too lazy, too busy playing video games, too selfish to lend a hand. She speaks to him as if he is a child and she is mama. He yells back about how incompetent she is. How he works hard all week to come home to this miserable rat hole and then get yelled at again. He will take out the garbage if and when he feels like it. (It piles up high before one of them gives in and both are miserable for several days and at odds with each other in other areas.)

A UF woman will recognize that it is a level one, and take it out herself. She lets level ones go. She is not petty over the small stuff. She sees it as good practice in case she ever has to do without him and as she goes past the garage he sees her, apologizes as he takes the trash from her. She says, it really was not a problem, she didn't mind taking it out that one time and was sure he had just forgotten to take it out. (Both are happy, neither feels put upon, and they are a team)

A level two hurt. They were shopping and came across a colleague from his job. He forgets to introduce his wife.

A worldly woman will assume that means he is going out on her. He doesn't want to introduce his wife because the office must know he has a lover. She accuses him of this in the car ride home, screams, rants, and starts packing her bags. He is at a loss for words. He is only forgetful and not good at the introduction thing but she takes everything he does wrong. After screaming for hours, she quits threatening to leave but still has her suspicions and plans to watch him like a hawk. (A very deadly aura is in the air and there is a lack of trust in the marriage).

A UF woman stops, thinks and categorizes. Yes, this is a medium hurt. She is a little ticked but not really emotionally harmed, but if she lets it go, it could add up and become a big thing. Better to let off some steam. She says nothing until after dinner. When he tells her what a delicious meal she prepared. As he kisses her on the cheek, she brings out the spice. She tells him that he should not kiss her like that because her husband would not like it. He turns around and looks at her with a strange expression.
"I am your husband", he says.
"Prove it", says she.
He moves in to hug her and she dodges him and warns him that her husband is big, strong and very jealous.
He tries to use his wedding band as proof.
"Nope", she has seen lots of men with rings.
"Well what would it take to prove to you I am your husband?" he finally gives in to the game.
"When you introduce me as such she says." as she walks away to the bedroom. When she almost reaches the door, she turns and looks at him and over her shoulder and sees he is coming. She says..."oh no, only my husband can be with me in this room." He takes her in his arms, assures her that he is her man and that he will never make the mistake he made today, ever again. She looks up at him and says...
"I thought you looked familiar". (All is good. She told him with sauciness, that he messed up and he loved how she told him).

Level 3 hurt. He forgets her birthday.

A worldly woman has had enough. She packs and leaves him to go to mothers. She has had enough of his forgetful ways and he obviously has a lover anyway. She saw him talking to that woman at work with the long legs and short skirt. It was a good thing she has been checking on him. Much better she know now. He comes home and sees she is gone and reads the long rambling letter she wrote listing all his supposed flaws. Yes, he did forget her birthday and he planned to make up for it tonight but the house is more peaceful now. Maybe it is better that she is gone. And she is right about one thing...there are plenty of women out there. (the beginning of the end).

Our UF woman is crushed. She has decided to use exaggeration to help him understand just how hurt she is. She keeps two things foremost in mind. That she accepts him no matter what along with his forgetfulness and that she chooses to be happy. She knows herself well enough to know that she can't let this go by without saying something or it will ferment and grow. She also realizes that she doesn't feel a need to punish him. That is not her choice, ever, but she does really need to let off some steam and for her, using exaggeration works the best.

She tells him that she is the most miserable creature in the world. She must be unloved. Why did he marry her? She is just not worth a little gift or even just a cake maybe a card...he could have made it on the computer, even but no, he didn't even acknowledge her special day at all. He should have left her in that restaurant he met her in. She thought all these years he adored her but he, the man she loves more than anyone else, didn't give her even a happy birthday wish. She is so miserable, she just wants to wear black all day and listen to jazz.

He is beside himself. He is so sorry to have forgotten. He begs her not to feel this way. He loves her. He wants to make this up to her. Will she go out with him tomorrow? No, she is just too sad. She walks into the bedroom. He follows and asks what she would like as a present. She tells him her birthday is over now and she doesn't need anything and she walks to her sewing room. Again he follows begging to know what he could do to make this up to her. She gives him a faint smile and walks out to her garden and tells him that she is the one at fault. She had to have done something to make him not want to remember her birthday. She picks flowers for the table as he follows behind her, offering her many things but especially his apology for a bad memory. She tells him not to worry. She will work harder to make him love her more. (This is called the chase in UF language. A man loves to chase a woman even after he has already caught her. I will leave it up to you to guess what wondrous things she was given when he came home the next night. Their home is happy, all is forgiven and he never forgets her birthday again.)

When I first suggested the above scenario on the list, some women were shocked at the suggestions. It seems all contrived and manipulative. I think there is validity in giving yourself a second to think about how important this is to you, a 1, 2, or 3 scale is good for doing this. It automatically helps you to let go of the petty stuff without even dwelling on it too much. It also gives you a way to let off some steam without letting it all build up which a problem many of us have, especially this red-headed wonder. Stop and think and try to come up with something a little spirited, a little saucy and a little fun and your life will be amazing.

Face the fact that men are different from women. That is a good thing, really! Knowing the basics of male/female interactions is a powerful thing to master. A man will react in manly ways, to a woman who needs his protection.

As a widow, I know that I am capable and able to take care of myself. The worst has happened for me. But I have learned that I can do quite well on my own. I am running a house, hiring things done as need be. The bills are getting paid and the essentials are being taken care of.

Since I have been in this situation for many months, I had forgotten some of the basics. I have become capable on my own and forgot to need. Let me tell you what happened.

Fairman invited me to dinner at his house. Yes, a man who cooks! How fortunate am I? After a beautiful dinner, we listened as his son, Jon played the piano and during this pleasant domestic picture of tranquility, a storm came up and the rain started to pour down. Fairman said: "Sandy, looks like you will have to stay later tonight than you normally do".

I forgot all my training, and all my study and proceeded to argue with him. I assured him that I wouldn't melt if I got wet. He told me that he would worry too much if I were out at night in the rain. Still, I let him know it was not the only time I had been in rain at night and I would be fine. He shook his head and I knew that conversation was over. I would give into what he wanted.

What I was saying in man-language was...I am a woman who doesn't need you, or your protectiveness...worse, I don't need you to care about me. I don't need you, at all. Really, that's what they hear when they offer a protective arm to a woman and she rebuffs them. This sweet loving man was telling me just how much he cared about me, about my welfare and I was in effect telling him that I didn't care what he thought, that I didn't need him.

Ouch! He did manage to get me to stay until after the rain storm because he was quiet and did not answer my arguments. He is a very good leader and knows how to direct me. Quite a skill when I can be so headstrong at times. As he walked me out to my car later that night, again he tried to show his care for me. "Sandy, please remember that the roads are wet and will be slippery. I know how you like to drive a little wild sometimes." Ohhh out came the mouth again...don't I know how to drive...I can manage just fine.

Well, on the way home, I was driving a bit too fast for the deep puddle I hit, Fairman's words still in my ear. I slowed down and thought about the night and it was finally then that I recognized that I had solicited a protective feeling in this man I loved. This was something I had wanted and had received without acknowledgement to him or myself. What an opportunity I had missed to praise his appreciation and care for me.

I wrote him an email the next day telling him how much I appreciated his being protective of me but it meant a lot less to him at that point, I am sure. If, instead, I had thanked him and assured him that I would do as he said, it would have been so much better for both of us. He would have basked in my appreciation of his protection and I would have reveled in being so cared for.

Does any of this sound familiar? It really is ok to let a man protect you. We live in a world where men so seldom are able to be the knight in shining armor. In UF, we call this "killing our own snakes". Sure, we can, but it does so much more for the relationship if we step back and allow him to protect. Men know that they are stronger, bigger and more able to protect. What they don't know is how to fight a woman to allow him to protect her. In the last few decades, society has dictated that we should be better men than men are. So much is lost when this goes on. Allowing him and appreciating him in the protector role is more suited to his gender and ours. He loves the feeling he gets when he is able to shield the one he loves for just one little worrisome thing. How he yearns to protect her from all things that would hurt her if only he could.

When a woman chooses a husband, she knows that he is a great man of character. She knows that he has faults maybe, but she chooses to not focus on those faults if she lives the UF life. If he has suggested that he wants to be better in a certain area, she would do well to help him. HOW?

By believing in him. For example, a man feels that he is not going to go higher in the company. In his deepest despair, he may have given up those feelings of doubt to the woman he loves and trusts. She supports and encourages him with words of belief in him, perhaps even words of belief in him being much more than he is. (caution, never say anything you don't mean...believe in him yourself and don't lie).

"Darling, you are the very best manager in that company! They know that they would be lost without you. You have always handled yourself very well and I just know that you will excel and come out looking better than ever. I could never imagine how you manage to handle all the things that you do but I am amazed and in awe at your ability."

He may argue with you. He may accept what you say. Regardless of how he handles those words...keep saying them. Keep believing in him and keep supporting him. The world is going to knock him around enough, and the last thing he needs is for the woman he loves and works so hard for, adding to the kicks!

If a man is given enough positive strokes at home he will claim the world. If he isn't, he will look for it somewhere, anywhere or he will go deep within himself out of the pain of a wife who judges him inadequate, not good enough. He wants so badly to make her life better and happier. When she is negative, he feels he has failed and his self-esteem plunges.

I know of a woman who had a husband that was just terrible at conversation. She started believing in him. She would listen to him as if he were already the most wonderful conversationalist in the world. She would tell friends within his ear shot about how good he was at conversing. And things changed. He really became quite good at talking with others. People started coming to her and telling her how much they enjoyed conversing with him. Believe in his positives and make them more!

Can we see this ideal in use outside the marriage arrangment? Yes, positive words to a child will always give the child a sense of self-worth. "If mom thinks I am something special...then I must be...moms know everything".

What about in our friendships? If a friend is going in a direction that is not beneficial to her, how can we handle it? UF is not necessarily a popular idea in the world. And even in our community here, we can see that all of us are at different levels. Some have accepted part of the ideals but not all of them. Some have accepted all of them but have not been able to live up to them (me included) and some ...it seems to be second nature to them and they are the poster wives/moms for UF.

We have to acknowledge this if we want to help a friend in the UF way. We can encourage all the positives in her life. We might suggest that this is something we have tried and she might just want to give it a try. "I have been making some gender studies and tried this once, why not try it yourself and let me know how it worked for you?"

Remember to encourage and support wherever you can. A friend was always surrounded by people who adored her. I finally figured out what was special about her. She openly told people what they did well. She would have young and old beaming as she told them how good they were, how strong, how special, how important they were in her life.

This is powerful stuff! I truly belief that we change the world for the better by living these ideals. Can you change the world this week within your small circle?

Chapter 3
She is Dependable

Two women came to my mind from my childhood. They were both in their 60's back then and best friends. One was a widow and the other still was married but did not drive. The one who drove would pick up her friend nearly every day to go somewhere, shopping, for lunch, or to church.

They were always dressed very nicely and completely. They would be wearing scarves, necklaces, earrings, bracelets, purses and shoes to match. I remember watching them at church wondering just how many pairs of shoes and purses they each owned. They wore a bit of lipstick and a bit of scent. I was with them once, when they were leaving church to go to a parade. They had brought walking shoes in little canvas bags to change from their church shoes. Often times they wore hats and gloves.

I never remember them wearing the same thing twice. I do remember always being intrigued and content to watch them. How they moved their hands, how they walked and carried themselves. How they spoke and laughed. They had their faults, they were both terrible gossips and they would often grumble at each other over trivial things. But they even did that in a dignified way. They were classy even when they were acting like cats. But it always ended with them laughing at each other and their silliness.

As I grew older, I would often be an invited guest in their respective homes. The one, Margarite, loved her animals, especially cho cho, her little dog, who would be talked to as if he were a child. I remember being served delicate little cookies and when I asked for the recipe, she told me that I would have to first go out and collect the rose petals. They were flavored with rose water and the recipe was very old. The house was full of antiques from her life and neat as a pin and lots of china cups and flowers about the place.

Margarite never seemed to stop moving and found humor in many areas. She took me out to her beautiful garden and laughed at a certain flower that always seemed to drop no matter how she tied it back. She laughed at it's being obstinately sad because it was jealous of other flowers.

Each time I had a new baby, later in life, Margarite would call my husband to come and get the antique cradle that had always been in the family. She said that we were her family too and that it was better for it to be used rather than in storage.

When I would go to visit Marge, I would feel a bit uncomfortable among the huge ferns and expensive collectibles and antique furniture. She served expensive goods from a bakery far from town. When you would admire some item displayed, she would say..."oh they are just things. People are what are important" She enjoyed hosting gatherings in her large home, including my bridal shower...it was a tea of course.

As these two ladies walked into old age, life changed for them but it only seemed to draw them closer. Marge, too found herself widowed. Margarite's eyes grew dim so that she finally had to give up her beloved driving. She kept her car so that they could ride in style with one of us who would volunteer to take them where they wished to go. Margarite left us first. After that, Marge moved into a brand new apartment in town so that she could walk for what she needed and be less of a burden on others. She continued to be classy right to the end. I remember a time when most days were spent in her bed as she lay dying from cancer. But out of town friends asked to take her out to dinner. She summoned her strength to enjoy that one last outing. It took her most of the day to get ready. A hair dresser came and worked magic on the thin hair. She looked spectacular, as she always did when her friends came to call for her. She made use of a walker but did so slowly, and with great posture seldom seen in a woman of that age. The husband of the couple walked her proudly to the car.

They enjoyed a wonderful dinner and she ate it all with relish although quite a bit of the meal lay hidden beneath a lettuce leaf and eventually her napkin. She entertained them with great stories and the latest gossip that she still managed to pick up from some where. But then she became quiet and the couple looked across at each other and knew that Marge had exhausted herself and it was time to go.

As the gentleman walked her slowly up the walk to her front door, she asked him if he minded stopping for a moment, just to enjoy the scent of the flowers...but he knew she just was too tired to go on. He offered to carry her in the rest of the way after some moments and she gratefully accepted, and as he laid her on her couch in the care of her nurse, she joked that it had been quite some years since she had a handsome gentleman carry her across a threshold.

She died later that week but I think that she passed away quietly and happy from that final outing ready to greet the next world in just the same dignified way, she left this old one.

How wonderful to be thought of as a woman of character, dependable and reliable. The highest compliment I ever received was from the wife of our priest. Some of you may remember my writing about being at the beside as a hospice volunteer when he passed away. The compliment she later gave me was this..."Sandy, no matter what you are doing, right down to the smallest thing, it is always obvious that you have a great love of your God."

She made this comment in a women's group meeting. It brought me to tears and made me really stop and think, how is it that I am reflecting spiritual things? What is making me seem that way to others? The answer to a large extend is UF.

To be a woman of character, you must have absolute faith. You must know that your belief is based on strong basics. You must never be afraid to let others know what your faith is because to be afraid is to be ashamed. That deep conviction of what one believes in gives you strength that can be unbelievable at times. It is a strength that can get you through the most trying tests. It can give you confidence in the face of adversity and calm in the middle of burning trials.

When you build up your character, you won't hesitate when there is a choice to be made. You will know that you must be able to face yourself in the mirror and not be ashamed. You know that many people look to your strength, even your husband and if you fall from grace, you fall from the pedestal he wants to keep you on forever.

If you show that you are unafraid to face the consequences of choosing the pure paths, then others will swarm towards you because they will know that you are a woman whom they can depend on, that you are a good faithful friend and truly a woman of character who will always be glad company.

If you choose to be strong against badness, even if ridiculed for it, those who would laugh will not stay in your company. Guess what? You don't want them around you anyway. They are not good and true friends. They are the kind that have no substance. Their laughter at your steadfast ways, will do them no good when hardships come and they need strength. Those who mock you will tend to try for easy ways out of trials and will find a lot of heartache instead. Much better that they laugh and find that you are not of their kind than for them to draw you into their heart cries later.

A woman of character will always be content with little and find a serenity that much of the world is missing. She knows that life is being directed and guided and that her course is plotted carefully. She doesn't have any need to be afraid. There is a quietness of heart, a spiritual aura, a sense of living graciously on the earth but perhaps partly in the heavens. She knows that she will always be provided for as long as she puts first things first. If her priorities are in order, there will be peace no matter what.

This is a healthy way to live. Studies have shown that those people who are adaptable, no matter what life gives them, tend to live longer. It is all the more important in the time we are living. Some very serious things have happened in the last few years and some of us feel we are living in the shadows of uncertainty.

We, the mothers and wives of this generation have seen much too much. We were there to aid and comfort and strengthen our families when we watched the towers come down and watched our children go off to war. We prayed for the families and tried to explain when our little ones questioned the death of a teacher and her co-workers from the

Challenger flight. We prayed even harder as the waves hit a coastline far from our home. And now, again, we pray for those who have been lost, those who are still lost and those who are searching.

We have watched the great storm come closer to the shore, sighed a bit of a relief when it seemed it was not all that bad, and then watched in grief as the totality of the devastation was revealed. And now it seems, that each one of us to lesser or greater extent, will be affected by the hurricane season of 2005.

That is the situation, as I see it right now. But through it all, we are women of great strength, integrity and character. I want to make some suggestions here about tangible things we can do, but I don't want those suggestions to let any of us lose sight of the true importance of our position in the family. To be the heart of the home, the comfort our family needs and the bringer of hopes.

You must understand that we, the mothers and the wives, we are the foundation of where our family will be, emotionally. We can strengthen the world by our hope and by our belief in our fellow human creatures regardless of the acts of a few who have strayed far from the golden rule. We can bring our family to a better view of the world by making their small home world secure, loving and full of good hope for the future.

How do we do that? Bake! Sing! Put a wooden bowl of fruit on the table. Get up from this book and turn off the TV, turn off the computer and do something right now to make your home a comfort. Decorate for the season. Put on some music. Make home life a true haven for your loved ones. They are going to come in from a chaotic world and need peace and order to get their bearings and to be able to go back out into it again, and again, day after day.

Bring out some games, cards, plan a picnic. Get their focus away from the horrors for as long as you can. Keep your fears to yourself but prepare for the worse as a capable wife would. Preserve food stuffs as you are able. Take to the yard sales of the season and get warm clothing ready for winter. It may be that we will need to keep warm with less fossil fuels. Since we obviously will be spending more time at home, consider some wholesome family activities. Invite close neighbors and friends over. By banding together, we also find comfort. Steer the conversations to positive things.

Remember that your character will keep you from panic. Don't be surprised if you find that people flock to you to borrow from your strength. Keep making comfort foods... soups, bread, cookies. When you get worried or heart sick, cook something, knit something, do something to make others more comfortable. That is how all our fore-mothers managed during the depression, during all hard times.

I believe in the ability that UF has to make a difference in the world. We do it by beginning with our family circle and we continue to widen out like a drop of water does as it causes ripples in a pond, until at last the whole world is better. We can do this! We can teach hope, and caring by living it.

In UF we teach something called the "Sacred Secret". Do you know what it is? Have you seen the glint of it in the eyes of a widow? Have you heard the murmurings whispered into a newborn's ear? One of the most important facets of a fascinating woman is her sacred secret...strength.

We know the secret. That we rely on the strong shoulders of our men to support our emotions, to lean on when the small trials of life try to weaken us. We draw on the strength that our men give to us daily to protect us from the dragons. The strength they have keeps us free from the pressures of fighting the rat race, of people who do not care about us or our needs. Our men brace themselves against a heavy wind of day to day stress that allows us to tend to our little comforts sheltered in his shadow, safe from the worries and strife he faces alone. This protection that a man offers is not appreciated by the modern woman. She pushes him aside and tells him she can handle the currents as well or better than he can. He presses on, confused by her dismissal, but presses on wanting only to shelter her from all harm. The burdens are even more heavy on his heart knowing that he has no choice but to fight against them but also knowing that he has less to fight for, no cause other than to do it while she competes with him.

UF has helped us to understand that he fights bravely and more proudly if he fights for us. It has helped us to understand that allowing him to face the onslaught also saves our strength for roles that we may need to take on later in life. He needs to know in his heart that should he lose his life before she does, that this love of his life will be able to take up the fight herself, strengthened by his shelter and care up until that point. He needs to know that she could carry on without him. He needs to know that all he loves and cares for in this world would be continued on with the strength he lends her now.

How does he know that the sacred secret of her strength will be there? She displays it day to day in her character and ability. When she comforts the depressed, she shows that she does not put herself first. When he sees her giving of herself to worthwhile pursuits and charities while still putting the family first, he sees her capability and spirit. When he sees that she is a rock of strength when called upon to defend, he sees the future strength she will have to endure the trials that life may place upon her.

Have you known women who have faced terrible dreadful sadnesses, and faced them bravely and with character? I watched the wife of our last priest say goodbye to him as he left this world. I stood guard over her room, giving her a few minutes alone with him while others due to their own sadness wanted to rush in and pour it out. For about a half hour, she talked quietly to him. I don't know what words she spoke since, she was in my vision but not my hearing, but I do know that she called upon the sacred secret and it did not fail her. She allowed those others to come in after a while and she was composed and strong and has remained so all this time. After I lost David, she came to me and gave me a safe spot to cry in her arms and I begged her to tell me how do you do this? She said: "Sometimes, you have to stop thinking about it for a while, but day by day it does get easier." She was right of course. We recognize the sacret secret of strength in each other and value it.

So let your husband shelter and protect you. It is what he needs to do with every pore of his body and every ounce of power in his soul. Each day he does this, he strengthens you. There will be days that he calls on you to pour some out on him as a refreshing drink on a hot day. He may need to let down his defenses just a tad and let you sympathize with his miseries. He may lose a parent and desperately need you to be strong enough for the two of you. He may take a hard blow like the loss of a job or a demotion or other arrow hurled towards him, to break him and bring him down. But he has you, he has aided the strength in you and you will be able to mend him and help him stand once again.

This is the power of the sexes and the perfection in the two becoming one. This is not about women being lowly humans and serving the man beast. This is about the give and take, the allowing each to do what they do best. This is about acknowledging who we are and how we are made and putting all things right for the strength of the whole of humanity. This is allowing him to be who he is so that you can become stronger day by day. We are all that is lovely and sweet and feminine but our husbands need to know, must know for their own sense of peace that if the worse should happen that you have a strength that probably far exceeds his own.

I recall a woman who ran over her own child with a very large lawn tractor. This mother managed to pull that tractor end over end to get it off this child. She was extremely feminine lifting all that weight. She was protecting her child.

I remember years ago, my own young child went into convulsions while sitting on his father's lap. I grabbed him, noted a fever and ran him into the bathtub to cool him which was the advice in those days. I held this child while he jerked and convulsed and ran water over him while his strong tall father stood there unable to move. I had to tell him 4 times to call for an ambulance. He finally muttered that he didn't know how. I screamed at him and ordered him to the phone to dial the operator and order an ambulance. Hearing his wife order and yell at him was so foreign to him that it knocked him out of his terror for our child and enabled him to act. Was that feminine? Yes, again, I was protecting a child and motivating a man to action. This was what he needed me to be.

I was in a car accident. A bad one with my mother driving and all of our 5 young children at the time, my daughter an infant. A split second after the crash, I checked all the children to make sure they were not harmed, saw that my mother was not able to get out but breathing and moving alright and then checked myself. There was blood all down my blouse, and some more clouding my vision and I was going to pass out soon. No pain but I had to find someone to hold my baby before I lost consciousness. And I managed it. My mother was extricated with no broken bones. I had some facial fractures and pulled the ligaments in my knee and ankle. Some plastic surgery and I was fine. How did I fight off shock and fainting long enough to see to everyone else? The sacred secret.

Here is the point...your husband needs to know that if you have to, you can be extremely strong. He has to know and feel secure in you, that should he not be there you can protect his children. It is a gift to him to know that if you should have to face the world alone without him, perhaps even have to do some things not comfortable for your gender, you could and would not hesitate.

I want to share something very personal now. As you know, my husband, David, lost his lifelong fight with depression. For many reasons, he chose to take his own life, and I have come to respect even this decision although if it had been in my hands, I would never have allowed it. It wasn't. He left a letter and this was part of his last words to me:
"Sandy

You did nothing wrong. You are much better than I ever deserved. The 6 years that we have been together have been the hi-light of my life. You are the only part of my life other than my children that has meant so much to me. Forgive me one last time, please. I love you and adore you. I pray to God, that He can make your life what I didn't. My last prayer to God is that he grant you the goodness, happiness and grace of life that you deserve."

I very much loved that man. It was so hard to carry on. To pull myself together and do the necessary things. The hardest thing was to carry on without him. But, I think that his prayer has gone answered. I have found a man who loves me and has given me all the things David wanted for me. I write this, dear reader, to let you know that I have lived what I preach and that I will always be thankful for knowing these secrets.

This is why UF women are so dependable and have such high standards. We are so above the minor issues. We live on a different plane.
If a man really loves you, he wants to sleep with you right away, right? So, a single woman gives in to (his) needs to fulfill her own and they live happily ever after, right? Not in the majority of the cases. Many men who will encourage this in you are the kind that want sex and not a relationship. They may even be the kind that want lots of women. It takes time for a relationship to blossom and sex can get in the way of really learning about each other.

A UF single woman will let all the men she dates know up front that she has standards. She will let them know before she goes out with any man that she is looking for the mate that she will be with the rest of her life. Believe me, this weeds out a goodly number of men before you even go out with them. But why set yourself up for months of heartache that will only be a waste of time that could be spent searching for the right man? Keep to your standards. Have them written down and if a man is slow in moving toward a relationship, kindly let him know that you have some standards for a mate and you are not sure that he knows what to do with a real woman now that he has found one. You surely don't want to waste his time or yours.

UF woman are not needy. We don't cling. If a man is not showing himself to be of the caliber deserving of a UF woman...put some distance between you and him. Give him the gift of missing you. What often happens is he will see what a jewel you are and will chase you to get back in your good graces. If he doesn't, he might not have been that into you anyway and pat yourself on the back for not wasting months or years on a dead-end relationship.

What about you married women? Do you still have your standards? Ultimately feminine are ladies. They deserve to be treated as such, especially in public. Most men worth anything at all will apologize quickly if a woman reacts to coarse words with "oh my" and look down quickly, especially if she has children with her. A 'sorry ma'am' is sure to follow and it should. You deserve to be spoken to like the princess you are.

There is also the pornography issue that affects so many marriages today. Please do not allow pornography to defile your home. Keep the computer in the living areas and monitor your young ones. A man and woman who are married lovers should not have separate passwords. Offer him yours as a sign of faith and trust and expect his. It is so easy for a man to think that he is an island and that no one knows what he is looking at or sharing or who he is flirting with. Discuss the subject openly. The danger is that what was once seen as thrilling becomes boring and a man can find himself looking for more and more to the point of endangering his relationship or worse.

You deserve to be the only one in his life to entice and thrill him romantically. Be sure that you are the one he comes to for this. Keep the motto...if my husband is going to have an affair, let it be with me. Be that for him. If he does slip, let him know just how disappointed you are and that you thought better of a man like him and that it definitely does affect your marriage.

I know of a story of a married couple. The man was getting towards middle age and romantic interludes were becoming more physically taxing for him. He turned towards pornography to aid him in this. His wife was very against such things so he became adept at hiding what he was doing and looking at. When she would awaken in the middle of the night to find him not in their bed, she would get up and see him on the computer. He would tell her that he couldn't sleep so he was looking at things on e-bay. She didn't know he had other things hidden under that e-bay screen.

One day there was a knock at the door and police came and seized the computer. The husband had been looking at child pornography. He tearfully explained to the wife how it had started out as simple pornography but got boring for him and he went looking for younger women. Two days after the knock on the door, she found her husband dead, hanging in the barn.

This may seem like an extreme story but it is happening. Remember that you are angels atop a pedestal. Please don't lower your standards because, you're keeping to them, may save so much more than your marriage. Understand that he wants and expects you to be more spiritual and more good to make him be a better man.

Being dependable applies to us as home makers as well. I recently had some contact with a young family member who easily went off the handle. She would shout others down. She would get suddenly angry if you did not agree with her and run to another room shouting at you as she went. A person could not get away with silence because this young woman would demand that you always take her side, always agree with how she saw life.

She seemed to need to use vulgar language to make her argument more valid and most of the time, it seemed she was arguing with no one. The person she was chatting with had no idea that she would react that way unless everything she said was completely agreed with. The people in her vicinity were caught off guard that an argument would so easily arise with her. It soon got to the point that no one really wanted to say anything to her, walking on glass shards to keep from upsetting her. And of course, this only made things worse because then people were ignoring her.

What words come to mind? Prima Donna, spoiled, bratty, self-centered? How different this is from a woman of excellence who works on ultimate femininity! A UF woman is interested in keeping peace centered about her. She desires a quiet home and she has a mild spirit. She prefers to let others feel they are right rather than pursue arguments which are based more on personal preferences.

The peace of her household is a daily goal. She works to make others feel comfortable with soothing words and encouragement. She values others, respects them enough to allow for their own views and opinions. All her words are chosen with care and thought out before said. She prefers to speak consoling words knowing that most of the time, critisism is not constructive to the person receiving it. She can be bold, if she feels the person hearing her words will benefit but again, it is with loving kindness that she speaks such words.

There are no doors being slammed, no angry words, no shouting directives at the children. There are good and happy sounds. Children are not screamed and threatened into bed. They are taken to bed, tucked in and stories and maybe songs are heard. Little prayers are heard.

There are no complaints, and outbursts when Daddy gets only one foot into the door. There are soothing sounds. Happy reunion sounds and sympathetic sounds too, when she knows he needs it.

This is your only chance in life to make a difference. You have been blessed with a home. It is up to you what you make of it. It seems so many women struggle with finding happiness in their work in the home. Some have been raised to see it as menial work for the lowly. Some become overwhelmed by what seems enormous work that never ends. Some just don't know how to do it. Others just have their priorities out of sync. UF is here to help and support.

Let's start with the homemaking aspect, which is only one facet of being workers at home. Is it menial? None of you see it that way but some of you may struggle with a past of viewing it like that or knowing that others, important in your life, do see it as menial work. They may ask suggestive comments about when you are going back to work or school. They might be questions like, "Aren't you bored doing nothing all day?" or, "Don't you feel like you are wasting your education?" or maybe even suggest that you should be doing more to make a difference in the world rather than wasting your time and talents watching soap operas and eating bon bons.

Remember that you are doing the most important work in the world by giving your family a haven of strength and stability. You are changing the world by making the ones you love stronger, most likely strong enough to go out into their environment and make a difference with those that they come in contact with day to day. You do make a difference. You are making an impact. No paid job is as important. OK, so cleaning the toilet may not feel all that fulfilling but if it is left undone, it could cause irritation and maybe even illness. My late husband was a supervising engineer but many times he made the comment that the person with the most important job at the plant was the custodian. He kept the plant comfortable and allowed the important work to go on.

By seeing to the human comforts, you show all who come into your home just how much you love your family. You show how important the people who come into your home are. They are given royal treatment. They are privileged to be in your home. It becomes a haven of rest and recreation. Everyone who steps over the threshold of your home is better for it because you are the heart of the home.

For a UF woman, the work is not overwhelming because she sees this job as a professional would. If she has not obtained the skills, and many young women haven't since Home Ec is no longer a subject in school, she studies and learns how to do the task at hand in the most professional way possible.

Unlike, popular home cleaning advice, a UF woman seeks to go about her home making as thoroughly and managed as she possibly can. She doesn't subscribe to doing any job half-way. She believes that she should go the extra mile because her family is worth nothing less. She seeks ways to simplify and streamline. She knows when to let go of something that is not making her home or family more comfortable. She is careful of the world's resources but she also knows that there is value to the floor space in her home and does not waste it storing not useful or ugly things. She uses all possible conveniences and technology that her ability and budget will allow.

We are professionals. We deserve to run our home in an efficient organized manner. In my opinion, this begins with a desk and files. For those of you who have secretarial jobs to do for your spouses which may include anything from a home business to the business affairs of the home, this central work station is all the more important.

Mine tends to get cluttered unfortunately and sometimes gets the nickname "Mount Desk". Start by getting the basics of home paper management, file drawers and file folders. Label them with every company that you do business with once a month and those that only come up a few times in the year.

Some home record keepers like to keep a tickler file with the 12 months of the year, and then days 1-31 files. Something that must be managed or paid or sent out on January 27 would be placed either in the month file or if you are already in January, in the 27th file.

Some of us have a computer at that desk that is not shared with any other member of the family. If your computer is shared by others, then make your desk separate from the computer desk. This needs to be your own space. It is also ideal if your spouse can have his own desk. If you must share this desk then opt for your own drawer or basket. Some women have managed to have a portable desk with writing supplies, notebooks and record journals that they can transport on and off a table.

I do hope you have your own desk though. This will be your place to plan the meals, shopping trips, homemaking schedules, manage the families appointments, plan the gardening and make business phone calls. It makes you feel as if you are in control. You are a professional in your home. This is also the perfect place for a vase for the first dandelion of the year, special artwork, little plaques from friends. Nice if you can have a reference library nearby in a bookshelf. This could hold a dictionary, cookbooks, (who says they have to be in the kitchen?), gardening, health and diet books, dollar stretching books, homemaking, cleaning, sewing and such.

I hope you have a homemaking book and at the very least a grocery price book that you have maintained listing the current prices for items you purchase.

You need a good calendar and/or software for organizing your days and weeks. I have had an appointment with caseworkers or for foster children every day for the last two weeks. If I didn't have some way to know who was coming over or where I was to have who and when...I would have been lost.

Some of you want to carry your scheduling info with you. I learned long ago to keep a datebook. Because it was too much to carry when I was dealing with diaper bags, I have gotten out the routine of carrying it. It is back with me and amazes me how often I turn to it when I am out. Some of you use palm pilots or other hand held computers for organizing. Well and good! We are living in a time of high technical improvements to our lives. Isn't it a good idea to maintain our old-fashion ideas of putting family first and giving the illusion of always being in control by making good use of things that we now have available. I would never do away with my dishwasher, computer or DVD player.

On the other hand, let's regain some things that make us more whole as gentle women who are happy in our gender. A beautiful pen (I prefer fountain pens) and feminine stationary to write real honest to goodness letters almost defines us. An online journal now called blogs are interesting, and I have toyed with placing one on my page at the website, but there is something so wonderful and romantic about a handwritten journal that can be passed on to future generations. Beautiful blank books with some pressed flowers maybe or sketches of wild flowers.

And while you are sitting at that desk of yours, I hope you have a window to look out and a comfy chair and maybe a tea cup waiting and cooling. I hope you have the first dandelion to make you smile and photos of those who love you to encourage you to finish your work because in actuality it is done for love of them and for feeling the validity of being a romantic woman.

Since UF women choose to be happy it also applies to the way they keep home. Sure there are some jobs that repeat and continue to seem redundant, but isn't that true of just about any important job? Some tasks are like that. So do them in as efficient a manner as can be managed in effort and time. Do them professionally. And find the positives. For a job that takes physical endurance like say, window washing, think about how you could be paying for the same sort of work out at a gym.

Are your priorities in order? I know of a situation where the homemaker would drop everything to help someone else. At first this sounds charitable but it wasn't because it was at the expense of her home and children for things not all that important. A neighbor ran out of napkins and this home maker would run to the store to pick them up which meant that her family had a very late dinner. Charity begins at home they say. Another woman was a bit of a social butterfly and loved to go shopping or out to lunch at the drop of a hat. Nothing wrong with that, in fact, UF encourages strong relationships with lady friends but this sort of socializing went on many times a week and her home and family suffered. If you want a well run home, you need to be at home often enough to see to it.

I respect any woman who is a part of our UF community and keeps her heart within her home, that has circumstances that make her need to work outside the home. She will always find support and encouragement here. She is in effect working two full-time jobs. I have the belief that if she is here among us, she has her values straight and knows that she will do what she can to make it back home as soon as she can.

That being said, I also want to acknowledge that being at home especially with little children, is not made easy in our day and time. The statistics are that only 30 percent do this now and that makes those special women a minority. It is not easy being different. It is important to find ways to find validation and support for this difficult work.

UF teaches that our husbands are to be made number one. We spoil them and support their careers. We make their at- home time special and a haven from the world. We understand that by doing this it is a strengthening bond that will in turn, strengthen our children. Seeing a strong united marriage is the best possible preparation you can give them. It will be a continuing source of strength as long as you are alive on this earth. Watching parents who love each other will prepare them to look for and encourage the same unity in their adult life.

We also endorse the thought that caring for our children and our homes and going the extra mile with this makes us care better for them and love them all the more. This gives us a fulfillment that is difficult to find anywhere else in the world.

But, with all this giving of ourselves it can become difficult to go forward day after day, unless we know the secret. The secret is filling our glass. Being a home worker allows this beautifully. I can take a bubble bath at 4 PM (Kelly Baths we call them), I can have a beautiful china cup full of strawberry tea and delicate little, expensive cookies and listen to Bach. I can enlist a sitter or swap services with a friend and go shopping for several hours alone once a week or month. I can have a planned rest day and stay in pajamas and read. I can have a spa day at home or if I can afford it out, I will. I can spend an hour of painting or crafts or sewing. I can have a picnic in the woods. I can plan all sorts of activities to feed my soul because I am my own boss. I plan my time and I acknowledge how important it is that I take care of my own needs.

UF women choose happy. They acknowledge that they are responsible for their own happiness and don't look for their husbands to feed that for them. They take charge of it. They know what makes them feel alive and happy and they owe it to their loved ones to provide it for themselves.

I love giving those precious few moments to my family in the evenings because I have had my time to watch TV or play video games or use the computer if it makes me happy. He can do what he likes. Hand him the remote and let him watch whatever he likes. Have an easy chair close to the computer so you can read and hold hands while he checks his email. Let him wind down how he likes. Be happy to see to his needs while he spends those few moments at home at night. The same with the children, if their mother has had a wonderful day doing some things that feed her soul, then how wonderful to come home to that mom; bet she even has some warm cookies and milk waiting for them!

Another part of home making is preparing healthy, delicious meals for the family. Yes, it must be both. You can make healthy food that no one likes and no one will eat and that won't put you any farther ahead. The goal is to have memorable meals without relying on convenient foods too much. Our worth in our home can be stolen by too much pizza or fast food drive bys.

Our family's appearance is a direct advertisement as to how much they are loved. Our family is royalty. They only deserve the best that can be afforded. Clothes should be clean and in good repair to the best of the budget's means. Haircuts should be a routine and if money is tight why not learn how to do this yourself?

As you get into a routine with your home making, you will find that you will do it better and quicker. One reason this is true is because doing it routinely will make less work. You don't have to think about it as much. Keeping up really is the key to finding more time. You will also become more professional in your attitude and the way you go about your tasks. Whenever someone tries to learn a new skill, they become faster as they become more proficient.

A word of warning though, please, please don't make your husband into the evil mean boss. Don't tell your children to hurry up and pick up because Daddy will be mad if they don't. Teach them to have their own routines and that they should be very proud of a job well done. You are the professional. No one should have to tell you what needs doing. You are the one in charge of the housework and you are the one responsible. If something is left undone, it comes back on you and makes you look bad since you are your own boss.

I am seeing a reaching back towards past times. College students are now learning to knit and crochet. These things have a calming influence and can give a huge sense of fulfillment. It is always a subject of conversation as well because when I am working on something, people will stop me to see what it is I am making. When you find that you have extra free minutes because you are such an expert homemaker, why not think about learning a new craft or art with the idea of it benefiting others?

When I was a girl, the exciting thing to do was to fly on a plane to Disney World and later Disneyland. But the real excitement was the plane ride. A man in a uniform would take your bags and make sure they were on the plane. You waited for a bit to get tickets and then you were told you could finally get on the plane.

The stewardess would smile and ask you if you would like to meet the captain and see the cockpit. The captain would shake your little hand and show you about all the controls and let you sit on his lap and look out over the nose of the plane. Then he would give you captain's wings to wear.

The excitement grew as the announcements were made and your parents belted you in and the plane took off! As soon as the plane was in the air, the stewardess would bring you something to drink and food on real plates on little trays that came down from the seat ahead of you. Later she brought blankets and pillows for dad to nap and special books for you to read.

That nostalgia is no more, as getting on a plane is all serious business these days. Security is first and foremost and though it is necessary, we have lost something special by gaining safety. Service is more likely a bag you pull yourself from a refrigerated box as you enter the plane.

A major New York newspaper reported the danger of living in the suburbs. What? Danger is supposed to be big city living. Nope, it seems that life in a development is detrimental to good health. In the city, people walk and exercise.
Many suburban homes do not have sidewalks and walking on fast roadways is a danger. Also there is longer time spent in a car because of longer commutes which adds stress to life.

What about the traditional family? Are they extinct? They are still there. Almost half of the mothers with preschool children are staying home with them or working part time. But if we take a closer look at how that family functions we will see a huge change from a couple generations back.

Children are to mingle. They are to get into school as soon as possible. From then on or even sooner they are involved in organized functions outside of home and school. Gymnastics, dance, Karate, soccer, baseball, football and any other number of sports leagues. They have play group and computer class and craft class and so much in other outside interests. Dinner is shared still but quite often it is the only meal that is shared and just as often it is fast food or prepared food heated in the microwave. Children are to be sophisticated, they date younger and younger every year. Schools begin parties and dances in early grades and then wonder why the kids are pairing off so young.

Mom is confused. She doesn't understand why she wants so badly to stay home but feels so little fulfillment when she does. Dad is baffled because he knows he SHOULD help out but doesn't know how and frankly doesn't feel good about doing chores at home. He muffs up quite a few of the chores and hears all about it later. He secretly wants to be taken care of and catered too like good ole dad but doesn't dare say so out loud. He works overtime to take away the confusion. He sees someone on the side to feel taken care of and catered too.

How are our little ones in suburbia turning out? Well they like to watch TV alot. Play a lot of video games and because they don't see dad much his guilt keeps them supplied with the latest gadgets. They like to eat while they do this. Eat and eat. They are pudgy and a little lazy and....yawn...it always seems like something is missing in life even though Mom and her taxi van carry them on never ending events.

Whew, this is all making me tired. Maybe we all need to just sit down and think about things a little more. Cook a real meal and read about simplifying and enjoying the little things. It's not hard to imagine a change for the better.

Chapter 4
She is Tolerant

When a person is not accepted then something in them is broken. A baby who is not welcome is ruined at the roots of his existence. These babies fail to thrive. Their heart is broken and their body follows suit when it gives in to infections or refuses to digest food. A student who doesn't feel accepted by his teacher probably won't progress well. I remember in fifth grade I had a teacher like that and my grades plummeted but went back up to A's when I found myself in my favorite teachers class in sixth grade. A man who doesn't feel accepted by his colleagues will perhaps suffer from stress illness and bring some of that lack of acceptance home.

There are stories of prisoners who gave in because of the misery of not being accepted. Acceptance is a basic human need. Acceptance means that the people in my circle give me a feeling of self-respect, a feeling that I am worthwhile. They show they are happy that I am in existence that I am who I am and they let me know that I am welcome to be myself in their presence.

If we choose to accept someone that doesn't mean we deny his defects or gloss over them. We know they are there. You can't really accept someone without accepting all of them good and bad. True happiness comes when you can make a difference in the life of another person and realize how much it really meant to them. Opening your hand to someone not only brightens their day but you also reap the benefits if only for a brief moment of true happiness.

What about accepting others in the religion they choose? Scary topic to take on isn't it? We know that it is politically correct to show acceptance of someone of another race or ethnic culture. We also know that the women on the UF list are UF sisters regardless of how much income their husbands or even the women themselves may bring in. It is easy to accept another even if her background is different. Even though often we feel close to the women

in this community it is a different matter to consider them as
sisters if they happen to be of a faith very different from ours.

Some of you know that this group had it's roots in the "Fascinating
Womanhood" movement based on a book by Mrs. Helen Andelin, a close
friend of mine. Many of you have read the book and though we differ
on a couple of points (mainly updates to the time we live) UF is
definitely influenced by Mrs. Andelin's studies.

A few years back a long time member wrote me asking me if I realized
that Mrs. Andelin was of a religion quite different from mainstream
Christianity. I was aware of her religious background...yes? This
longtime member was so distraught over it, that she left the
community and got rid of all Mrs. Andelin's books. I found it sad. I
wanted to ask her if she knew and approved of every actor that she
brought into the livingroom via the TV? Did she look into the faith
of all the musicians she listened to? Did she judge her Doctor's and
Dentists abilities due to the religion they were born into? How did
God view her bias towards only those who measured up to what she felt
was the true and acceptable religions?

I will send this to the Christians on this list now because they are
in the majority...What would Jesus do? He did make judgment calls on
the Pharisees and Sadducees, but it was not due to their being Jewish,
it was because they were hypocritical, telling the people one thing
and doing another. Christ was an example in accepting people of all
faiths and so should we be.

To those of you of faiths other than Christian, you also must
keep your tact and remember that many of us must learn how to be
accepting. Most of us were born into the religion we are in. It seems
a comfortable acceptable place and it is not something we give much
thought to. Often we just expect that others will see it as it is to
us.

My children have asked me my religious philosophy (yes, I do belong to
a mainstay Christian church, but that was not always the case). There
are two things I am personally sure of...There is a God ...and I am
not Him. Understanding this has kept me open to all sorts of people
and their religious choices. I am quite sure that I can learn

something from every religion on earth and all members of those religions. I am certain that God can use them as earthly angels sent to me to help me on this earthly course...that is if I don't judge them harshly and as unworthy. Who am I to decide who has favor and who doesn't?

This simple illustration has helped me a great deal over the years. Imagine a huge mountain and all the people are climbing up. Some are up towards the top, some are just starting out at the bottom. Most are climbing higher, some are slipping down a bit. Some are yelling to others, no not that way...don't go up that path, mine is better. Some are laughing when others slip down, some are speaking encouraging words to them...get up, keep going, you can do it!

Today, when you go about your day, please think about how you as a UF woman intend to climb that mountain and how you intend to speak to others on their own paths as well.

When I was doing foster care, the majority of my children were African American. It wasn't that there were all that many in care, there weren't. This culture normally takes care of their own and family or good friends will step in when a child is in need. The few that were in care in my county were normally sent to me because I had the knowledge of their special skin and hair care. I could braid hair.

In the African American people, a great man named Martin Luther King lived back in the 1960's. I was young when he was killed but I do remember him. I remember hearing his "I have a Dream" speech on the news. I didn't understand what he was talking about but I was mesmerized by his voice. I remember the little girl being led by the hand into school while people were angry and shouting around her. I was scared for her. I didn't understand. I thought that they were going to hurt her. As an adult, I know now that they wanted to.

I grew up in an area of the north where there were not many black folks. I remember one boy of color in my graduating class of 600. I remember hearing the N word when Mr. King was killed. Some of my dad's friends seemed pleased that he was killed. I didn't understand why and no one gave me a good answer. Was this a bad man? Race didn't really enter my mind as a reason. Perhaps it is true that children are color blind.

When I was a bit older, there were riots in Detroit which was an hour away. Race riots? Why? That's all I can remember about it...why? Again, I was afraid for the people who wanted to hurt others. It came across our new color tv set in the vivid reds of the flames of Detroit burning. Everything seemed to be about color. There was not much taught about any of this in high school history classes. Just like the Vietnam war, those years were echoes of silence.

Then I grew up and raised a family. We gained some diversity by living in Texas and Puerto Rico. We thrived with the cultural differences and I learned to cook new recipes and embrace the music and styles and cultures and bring them into our own realm. But still there were things that we knew were wrong but were helpless to change. Like the middle sized city that we lived in got rid of all their school busses so they would not have to go along with federal law to bus children into diversity. I spoke out against it to many who would listen.

It became almost pride that I was not bigoted. Then we went to foster training one night and were asked to try an exercise. We were given a bunch of marbles and a white plastic bowl. There were a lot of white, brown, yellow and black marbles each to represent the races.

First we were asked to place marbles in the bowl to represent the members of our family. Then we were asked to drop in a marble of a race that we would be willing to foster. We were told to chose a black marble if we were open to any race. We chose a black marble. Then we were asked to place a marble representing the race of each of the following:
Our religious leader
Our doctor
Our dentist
Our lawyer
Our hair dresser
Our best friends
Our children's teachers
Our neighbors to the right and left
Our neighbors across the street
and several others.

You guessed it. That poor little black marble was looking pretty lonely in there. No we didn't go out to chase down ethnic families and beg them to become friends but I did become quite close to the case workers and other foster families who have given me support in parenting little ones of another race. We would meet with a heartfelt hug and I am so very pleased to have them in my life.

Not to mention these little black princesses who have come into our life. But you know, even at their ages, it has infiltrated. We were discussing a certain worker and my 5-year-old said, is she the one that is a little bit black like me? I smiled and expressed surprise. This was the first time that I was aware that she was. I took the opportunity to ask her what her feelings were about white people. Ohhh she didn't like white people! I said, but Daddy and I are white. She said, oh no...you and daddy are pink! She came to terms with negative things she had heard by making us a different color because she loved us.

Having come to have children who are only here because their ancesters were stolen and made into slaves, I want to make it up to them some how. They are too young to know the history. A big part of me wants to keep the ugly truth away from them. And yet, maybe it is enough that I love them for who they are and maybe I can break them away from the legacy of pain that was their history by the bond we hold now. But history can't be re-written and gradually the truth will be absorbed as it was for me, little by little until this day.

So, here we are. A generation away from when a great man died but kept a dream alive. It may be that his dream is not completely fulfilled but each of us can do what we can to love across cultures and race. We can teach our children to love the differences by setting the example. Here is an essay that I wrote for the foster parent association back then:

I am a foster mom. How will you know? It isn't that I will tell you because I keep the privacy of the children I have, sacred. You might be able to recognize me though. I am a different race than the children who hug my neck and tell me at least 10 times a day that they love me. I am pushing middle age but driving to appointments with a diaper bag and sipping from a juice box singing "Jesus loves me" with background singers in assorted car seats. I volunteer at head start and when the children ask, "is that your mom?" my darling girl says with pride "oh no, that's my Miss Sandy".

They have a mom, but I am their Miss Sandy. My husband is Daddy. Sometimes, I am called Mom on the weekends when one of our respites (these are children who are from other foster homes but they come regularly to visit us to give their foster family a break) come to visit. Then there may be another race embraced and we do get some strange looks when all these little ones call us by their chosen title. We have our favorite restaurant to go to for breakfast before church. Our waitress is ready with her one question...how many do you have with you today, Mrs. Schindler...and then she is off to find crayons and coloring books. It is our routine. Our kids thrive on the routine. The waitress fusses over each child, telling them how nice they look.

I am never away from a phone and find myself saying more often than I like, "I am sorry but I am at my limit". Sometimes I am locked in the bathroom so little ears can't hear that mom won't be there for the visit and you hope that they are young enough that they don't realize the time for the visit went by. I call my husband at work and he always says that we need to be there for these little ones when mom can't be. We mourn together a loss that hopefully the kids aren't aware of.

If you come to my house, you will find toy land in our living room. Toys don't go in the bedrooms because we need to supervise troubled children who have not had a wonderful life and may not know how to play or may not know how to be nice to others yet. You will see bunk beds and highchairs and cribs. You will see nitendo games and a bunch of bikes. When I go garage sailing alone, I will make an offer for the whole load of toys or coats or bikes and when I explain that I do foster care, more often than not, people are generous with their price. They will tell me that they could never do that.

The church is always ready to aid us. Once we had a young man come to be with us on his birthday. A cake was produced and the song was sung to him, all these strangers who have become our extended family. The teachers in Sunday School who are always available to accept another and quickly learn names and make them feel like they have always been going there. The Priest gave us a blessing as we began this new ministry and the blessing has spread to all the little ones who have found us. I keep the written blessing framed on the wall. There are members of the church who wrap presents for children only after calling and asking "how many do you have this year for Christmas?".

My adult children do the same, leaving presents in strategic paper so I will know if it can go for a girl or boy. They support me in this but sometimes say things like, "Mom, why don't you go out and get a regular job so you can relax a little". I just smile. Some think that there is good money to be made doing foster care. There isn't. There is no amount of money I could spend elsewhere to equal 10 "I-love-yous" a day, though.

I did find that life changed after we took in children. Our friends are at the stage where they have grandchildren but are glad to see them go. They go to the opera and on cruise ships. We didn't get invited to go out to dinner or to visit their homes after we were accepted as foster parents. We also found that it was difficult to find friends our children's ages because we were going to be older than the family who might have them. I am finding myself, in between stages. Our friends became other people who are doing the same thing, this taking in of children. We go down our list of foster buddies when things come close to the surface. Those friends are always ready to listen without judgment. Close relationships are formed with the case workers and therapists of our kids. Who would have guessed. We even find parental feelings for the moms of our kids. Relationships all built on a love for children.

Sometimes people whisper to me..."why are your kids always so happy? If someone had taken my kids away, they would be crying all the time." Then I explain that these are children who are getting food on a regular basis. They have pretty clothes to chose from. They have toys and a regular routine. They have a bed and a home to live in. They have two parents. These are all things that most children take for granted. Our kids don't. They often sing to us...Thanks for spoiling us rotten. They mean it. And all they are getting are the things that other kids expect.

And when I hear for the hundredth time, "I could never do that." I think yes, you are probably right. You have to see it as a ministry to love and teach a child to love you back and trust you and know that you will one day have to give that child away. Maybe the court will order the child back to a mother who has done all the things required but still doesn't have the ability to keep those kids from coming back to you again in six months. You cheer her on, in spite of it. You prepare the kids to go back but this time they are stronger and have a voice. And if they don't go back into the system, you have given them an image to take into adulthood of the way life is supposed to be. It may be something that will keep them going.

Maybe you will have to prepare them to be loved in a forever family and have to answer why it is best to not let them stay with you. Then cry all night because you want to do the selfish thing and keep this kid instead of what is really right for the child. And you answer your own questions about who could possibly love this child more than you do when you know the answer is...anyone who knows her. So you do the best you can for them while you have them but also hold a bit for yourself because you know what is to come.

I am pleased when I hear a 5-year-old tell me that she will have a husband who loves her, like Daddy loves me and she will be a good kind of mom. And just when I start to tear up from a hundred emotions, her little sister will pipe up that she wants to grow up and be a dog. And you laugh and cry. That's what being a foster mom is.

So that was my big lesson in diversity, in learning to be tolerant of those different from me. I hope I learned it well and I hope I can pass it on to you. It is really something that is done for me, this acceptance thing. It makes me happy and secure. It shows me that people will become just what you expect of them. Sure I had some who gave me bad looks when I had this parade of children of different races toddling behind. I had a woman who was African American tell me how wrong I was for having these children. She told me how much better off they would be if they were with their own people. I agreed with her. I told her I was doing the very best that I could and they really deserved to be with their own people but there just were not enough homes for them in the African American community. I then suggested that she should open her home.

More often though, I received kind accepting remarks about the fine job I was doing. One who was the same race as my children thanked me over and over in the check out line at the grocery store. She blessed my efforts and complimented me on how well the children were looking and behaving.

Do you find it easy to accept people of a different age than you? Older folks really seem to have trouble being tolerant of teen-agers sometimes. As I grow older, I have learned to play a little game. I will watch music videos or find out what is in their teen lives or sometimes use some fad words just to get their attention. They never expect it and always makes them laugh. That little common bond breaks the generation gap and we are instantly gaining a bond with each other. I carry hip electronic equipment which also gets their attention. Asking them loaded questions that will bring out their opinion is a good way to get them talking. Young people are often very concerned about current events and problems facing the world. They often have a fresh insight that will surprise you and make you think. What a shame it would be to lose out on all of this because you aren't comfortable with that age. What about people who have passed the middle age mark? Is it hard to find common ground with the older folk? Have some questions about their life. The first time they were in a car, what was it like to see TV for the first time? Did they think it would catch on? What is the biggest changes seen during their life. You can glean so much information and learn from being in their presence. They won't be on this world much longer so time is short. Learn all that you can. Think of this when you see wrinkled brows. Know that this is a treasure that you should not lose out on.

I see my job as one that should open your horizons. Make you see things that easily could go past. Help you to be the most, the best that you can be. Life is short. Things happen that will surprise you. Take advantage of every single opportunity that comes your way. Don't let fear of the unknown get in your way. Embrace the differences!

Heartprints

Whatever our hands touch---
We leave fingerprints! On walls, on furniture,
On doorknobs, dishes, books,
As we touch we leave our identity.

Oh please, where ever I go today,
Help me leave heartprints!
Heartprints of compassion
Of understanding and love.
Heartprints of kindness
And genuine concern.

May my heart touch a lonely neighbor
Or a runaway daughter,
Or an anxious mother,
Or, perhaps, a dear friend!

I shall go out today
To leave heartprints,
And if someone should say
"I felt your touch,"

May that one sense be…YOUR LOVE
Touching through ME.
Author Unknown

Chapter 5
She is nurturing

When a baby girl is born, she learns from her mother's lap about the world. When she cries her mother holds and comforts her. The two of them have a secret language. I don't remember that time but my mother had 4 other children, two after I was in my teens. She taught them a lovey sound and would rock or pat their back to a singsong oh-oh-oh-oh. Sometimes she would stroke their little cheeks and sing. It was baby language for "I love you, so." She must have first taught it to me because I knew the song.

As a little girl grows away from her mother a bit and begins to explore her world, she imitates the loving nurturing she was given. My three-year-old does that now. Carrying her baby doll, rocking her, covering her with a blanket and giving her a bottle. She talks and sings and repeats the oh-oh-oh song, that I taught her when she first came to me.

Perhaps there is a little puppy that is brought into the household and she loves that little doggie and spends time brushing, feeding and caring for him many hours every day. It is sweet to watch her sing little songs to him or scold him gently when he has been naughty but still forgives him and throws her arms about his neck, even so.

School days bring about the nurturing of friendships. Special petals of heart songs different from the one learned from mother. There is sharing and secrets and memories that are sweet and nurturing. There are special times and friendships grow and become all the more close as the years pass.

And later, when she falls in love, she knows how to nurture the relationship by giving much more than she takes. She looks for ways to make him more comfortable and happy. She loves him and adjusts to his needs. And she longs for the day that the love they have will grow to embrace a new life.

When that baby comes, she nurtures him and cares for him and finds herself singing those little songs. She teaches him to love by the way she loves him. She has made the world a better place by raising a child who is secure and happy and all too soon, he too leaves the nest, just like she did.

But is she empty? No, she has found ways to nurture her friends who are there growing old with her. She has her little flower garden and babies her roses so that they grow more beautiful each year. Now that she has more time, she nurtures the world by giving of her time and talents to those more needy and she devotes her life to spiritual things and finds all the more to nurture in the service.

I think that each one of us can find ourselves in this place somewhere. Nurturing is a very feminine trait and the more we give the more we receive day by day.

Sometimes, people ask me why I continued to offer foster care. Why did I continue to mother long past the point most people do. For me, it was a ministry. I could have been leading youth groups or visiting shut-ins but this vocation seems to speak to me. It is my way of making a difference in the world and I am not afraid to tell you that it fulfills a great need in me, that I think lies within every woman's heart if she will just admit to it. A need to nurture!

It is always there if you look for it. The business woman who tends to her plants and the needs of each and every business contact. The old woman who lives with 20 cats needs to nurture, to baby. There is that neighbor down the road whose yard is overflowing with flowers and plants. The woman with no children who talks baby talk to her little dog. The woman whose children have grown and moved far away but she treats all the neighbor children to home baked cookies and has candy in her purse for each child at church.

Acknowledge this in yourself and accept the outlets that you use. It will make you a happier woman. Know that it is alright, that we are giving you permission to nurture others or things. This is a huge part of being feminine. Yes, there are some men who are nurturers but the trait is greatest in women. David was a great Dad but for the most part, he revisited his childhood with the kids and sometimes stirred them up in hilarious rebellions. He was the evil troll who likes to eat little children; some ears taste like roast beef and some ears taste like chicken. There is much squealing and hiding and running about when the evil troll comes to our house.

I am doing the nurturing, the band-aids on boo boos and the cleaning and the changing and the feeding. The little hugs and the smiles and the ability to fix anything, is very wonderful for me. I get the compliments when I take them out, girls dressed like girls and boys like boys, well behaved and polite. That comes from a lot of hard work and practice at home. The children thrive on positive words and that makes it worth the effort that the children and I put into it.

I don't have all the answers on parenting. I have raised my three, helped with David's two, opened my home to 25 children and had 5 live with me long term. Fostering is supposed to be professional parenting, but the only piece of advice I can give is....listen to your heart and it will tell you what you need to do. Don't let your children raise you, be the one in charge with Daddy being the only veto. He is the king of the house and what he says stands. The kids will thrive if you do that.

And enjoy them. Those little cookie monsters turn into lanky giants before you know it! Your parenting will change as they get into their teens. You will not need to modify behavior so much as lead and direct. Be open, allow them to know that what they have to say is important. I know that I sat at the kitchen table with cups of tea many hours while Andrea was growing up, just listening. I normally had to go and find the boys and listen to them while they were working on cars or sometimes over a game of cards. Listen, be there for them so that if they find themselves in over their head (perhaps I should say "when" because most teens do) that they know they can approach you. Sometimes they would ask me to be an ambassador between them and their dad. An important role because it showed that they did respect his position.

So, each woman here is in a process of mothering, care-taking, nurturing.

Embrace that all the more. It is healthy and important to the emotional needs of each of us.

Some have asked my opinion on home schooling. My children are in their mid-20's now and it has been long, long time ago since I did home school.

The mother who dedicates herself to this goal is a volunteer who makes the choice to educate her own children. I have always said that I don't recommend it because if you need me to tell you to do it, it probably is not something you should do. It is a heart choice that seems to come from within deep of oneself.

Let me tell you how I became a home schooling mom back in the days when there were no good laws on the books for it and some parents were being imprisoned over it. My first-born son was precocious. He was/is very intelligent. I am not exaggerating when I tell you that he could read by the age of two. It started out as a game the two of us would have after his sister took her nap. We would give each letter a personality, draw a little face in it and give it a name...A is the Andrea letter, Big B, C the candy man etc. He soon learned he had 26 friends and their children, the baby letters. We practiced how they talked...S says sssssss. etc.

Well, what can you do when your kid knows all the letters and all the sounds but teach him to read. So I did. We had fun. His sister wanted to know the 26 friends too before long and she was reading, later their little brother did the same. My children do not recall learning how to read. They were too young.

Then came the time for DJ to go to school. I called the school to see if they could test him because he was reading third grade books by then. They informed me that there was no way that they would take him that year because his birthday was one day under the age they accepted and he would have to wait until he was 6. I also learned that there would be no special provisions made for his level and that they did not have buses and we lived 8 miles away. The next year he was reading fifth grade level, I had a new baby and well, the law in Texas said that you did not HAVE to send them until they were 7. By then we were having fun with our daily learning time. The kids were getting so interesting that I thought they were doing better with me than they would have at school any way. We had lots of friends and they were getting plenty of social activities. About that time I began actively looking into the legalities of home schooling.

We took a lot of flack. People told me straight out that my children would be imbeciles and unprepared for the world of work. They didn't. They are in sales and in management making good checks. But I did worry. I had lots of self-doubts about whether I was doing the right thing or harming them. But it also seemed natural to me to be their teacher in life. I loved teaching them and watching them learn and they seemed to thrive. Two of them went and took the GED after they turned 18 and tested very high. So it seems that their education was more than acceptable. We learned a lot about life because we had a bit more time to explore. I feel very blessed to have gone through getting an education 4 times! I learned math skills and other things that I didn't get all that well the first time around.

The mechanics of it was different according to where we lived. When I was really fortunate, I had an extra room just for home schooling, but sometimes we had to resort to bins and the kitchen table. It really was a blessing for us and a time I look back on fondly and I think so do they.

Is it for you? Probably not unless you feel called to do it. Is it the best or the worse? Neither. Do you have to home school to do the best for your child? No, I think there are some mothers that just are not equipped to be their children's teacher and some children who will do better in the structure. It just worked out for us.

If you are home schooling or are looking to home school, we do have some support groups for UF members. Please see the website for more information. If this something that you chose to do, I will tell you that I found it filled a nurturing part of me. Teaching a child bonds in a way that is hard to surpass.

There is a special tie between mother and daughter. I want to really encourage you to build that bond so that this little girl doesn't have any doubt about the wonders of being born female. She will thrive and be secure in her role and bring that into her adult life.

Plan some special sharing for the girls and encourage male bonding between Dad and his sons. I would take afternoon tea with Andrea as often as we could carve out the time. I also enjoyed this ceremony with Dannielle, my step-daughter when she became old enough to carry conversations with. It drew us close and many secrets were shared during those special times.

I also would have a craft night with my foster girls once a week. We would create presents for teachers and friends and it also drew us close. Sometimes we would do a housecleaning with all the girls and I in aprons. The apron drawer also was opened when we baked. How many patty cakes went into loaves of bread or batches of cookies is anyone's guess.

I remember bonding with my grandmother as I learned how to knit and crochet by her side. She was all excited when I got a row finished, almost as much as I was. This was such a special memory and deserves to be carried out as an heirloom gift to children in my life.

Another sweet tradition borrowed from past generations is the hope chest. This was something that mother and daughter worked together on and dreamed about with visions of a future happy domestic life.

I did have one and so did my daughter. Mine continued to be filled right up until I got married and I remember all the shower gifts on it and around it. In those days, it was a sneaky way for mothers to teach their daughters fine needle crafts. I remember my mother handing me appliances that she no longer wanted for me to put in my hope chest.

But you know, times are changing. We can get nice sometimes unused things very inexpensively at yard sales and such. I would suggest that a girl in her late teens work towards that and decorate an old trunk or cedar chest. If you start too young, then the girl will have a warehouse for future home in her room and that is not logical...but small delicate things that she made or maybe her mother made to dress up her home with, would be wonderful. Perhaps you both could make her first aprons...one for use and one for her hope chest? UF advocates teaching the younger generation any handicraft and needle skill that we can. It bonds and it keeps them from being ":lost arts". You can teach femininity by placing some delicate handkerchiefs that belonged to her great grand mother. When we were girls our hope chests were something we shared with other girls....imagine her displaying that delicate bit of homemade lace to her friends.

So many of these lost traditions had other values to them...bonding mother and daughter, teaching femininity and self worth, encouraging her to be chaste until marriage by looking forward to it being special...hoped for. Teaching her to prepare for the future like the proverbs wife. Handing down family treasures.

Another good bonding opportunity is to make slippers. In oriental lands shoes are never worn in the house. It only makes sense since sleeping mats are used on the floor and who wants to sleep on dirt tracked in from the street? It is easier to keep floors tidy and clean if shoes are removed at the door. And most of our children love to sit on the carpet to watch television or play with toys.

I grew up in Michigan where there were mud rooms to take boots off before going into the house. It was common courtesy to remove your boots or shoes in the winter and not be tracking the snow, road salt or mud in on carpeted floors. We almost all had floor coverings to fight against the cold Michigan winters.

We wore slippers or "house shoes" inside. I used to knit or crochet pairs of them and place them in little bags with bows on to present to guests who did not bring slippers and were in stocking feet. Even in school we would take off our boots and dry them by the register vents between recesses. Some of us remember carrying our shoe bags with us. We wore boots and took our school shoes along in a bag but most of us stayed in stocking feet while we learned our lessons.

I know that some of you are followers of flylady.com (tm). She insists on shoes with laces to wear only in the house. The principle is still there. I seem to manage to get things done without the laces but our mentality about going the second mile and being fussy with our homemaking isn't exactly her standards either. I prefer house shoes or handmade slippers. It is a simple matter to slip my shoes off at the door and slip into the comfort and clean shoes.

We keep a mat on the inside and outside of the front door and we keep a basket for shoes. My mentality is to make it easiest to put away because the inclination is less than it is for finding shoes. In other words, my kids are more likely to toss the shoes into a box than put them neatly in a shoe rack in their closet. Digging the shoes out is more difficult but they have more incentive to dig them out because they have somewhere they want to go. Make the easier chore the one with the less incentive.

Take care of yourself. Pamper yourself with warm feet. Have pretty slippers to slip into first thing in the morning and when you return home to your haven. Encourage the children to put slippers on and take off their shoes at the door. Take slippers with you when you go to visit the homes of friends and relatives. If you ask at the door, "May I take off my shoes?" with your slippers in hand, it makes your hostess feel that you are comfortable and at home in her home and it can also keep awkward moments from happening when a family has a policy of "no shoes in the house".

And then there is the symbolic meaning of showing Dad to his chair with feet on the footstool and a member of the family undoing his shoes and placing warm comfy slippers on his poor tired soles.

Why not get some slippers for each member of the family or better yet...make some. I remember being 4 years old and receiving a gift of handmade slippers from an elderly friend of the family. They were made from the yarn that variegates into lots of different colors. I loved those slippers and they obviously made an impact on me to have them one of my earliest memories.

Do you garden? Many fulfill their nurturing needs by tending to tender plants, flowers, and vegetables. My first garden was some potatoes and I was thrilled with them. They were too much in the shade but still produced some new potatoes. I remember carrying that heavy watering can to them and being mesmerized by the daily growth. I remember how excited I was when Dad finally came with the shovel to dig them up. And I remember feeling like I was a part of a miracle when I saw that I had been a big part of dinner that night.

Pets fill that need in other of our lady friends. They bathe and cuddle and groom their "babies". I told you about my friend Margarite and her little dog Choo Choo. She would talk to that little dog as if he were human and he would react to her words. She truly loved that little dog and he loved her.

I have a cat named Rocky who is the recipient of most of my nurturing needs these days. Rocky is a blue cat who is very personable and vocal. When I ask him questions he always responds to me in his cat speak. He also lets me know when he wants something with his meows. His basic requests are "please give me food", "please let me go out to play in the yard" and "please cuddle me". Since he and I understand each other and our respective needs, it is not hard to make a guess about which of his 3 requests he may be making, which of course, gives the appearance that I understand the cat words. He also is given to making political statements which others may consider "accidents". His are political statements because they only happen when he has become displeased. I go on vacation and have Andrea come in and look after him and he will be sure to leave me political opinions like on my bathroom rug. After I come home he will continue to leave complaints unless I pick him up, show him the "opinion" and tell him, "no, bad cat, no more!" in a more elevated tone of voice than he cares for. He will sulk but he will stop with the politics.

He is also very loving. When he wants a cuddle, he stretches out so he can nuzzle my neck and run his paws in my long hair. He will grab it with his paws or pat my cheek, purring loudly in my ear. This is always on his terms, of course. He is after all, a cat. But if he decides it is time for a cuddle, he will be very vocal until I finally take time out to take care of his need for affection. This cat feels that the bathtub is not a safe place for me and yowls long and loud until he can finally rescue me from the evil thing. And his religious choice is pagan because I can play any music except Christmas music on the organ or CD's.

Tend to a live thing and give it love and care and you will be the one who benefits the most.

Chapter 6
She Celebrates

I ended the chapter on Romance and Celebrations in the book "*Ultimate Femininity*" with these words:

"So, I am suggesting that the woman has the responsibility for the continuity of life, not just because she is the child bearer. She is the keeper of the traditions, the celebrator, the rememberer. She is the one that encourages the routines of life. She is the one who remembers the romance of the ages. She makes life wonderful and full of memories that her children and their children will take into future generations. Make memories for them. They are your legacy.

Celebrate everything! Dad got a promotion, Johnny got an A, it's back to school time, it is home for the summer time, it is a party waiting to happen if you see it as such. When I was a little girl I loved making parties. It was my favorite game to play. I think that is why I see life as such a celebration. It is all a grand party and God invited us to this festival at birth!"

There are going to be sad times. I have had more than my share. Mourn those loses and then go on. Celebrate life because it is short and it is the best way to live those short days. When one celebration is coming to an end, plan the next one. A lot of the enjoyment is in the planning of this goal of bringing happiness to others.

My daughter tried to warn my fiancé, Fairman about how I am about Christmas. He defended me because he is just so gallant but he does now admit that she has a point. We have three Christmas trees and decorations wherever the eye falls. I think he has come over to my side though. His front yard is the only one within that Florida suburb that has pink flamingos pulling Santa's sled. Rudolf is looking on in disturbed shock. I love that man!

Traditions are such a comfort to the family. It shows that home is dependable and you know what to expect. The outside world is not like that at all. Add a little twist or something unique just to keep them guessing. Have those dependable traditions but make them wonder just what you might do next.

So why make a big deal over celebrátions? There is a good amount of homemaking that is quite repetitive. Making changes in the home feeds the creative soul, helps mark the passing of time and gives a built in goal to the routines. It encourages the homemaker to stretch herself and put herself on display. It is really a part of her personality that she is sharing almost like an artist does with paintings. There is also a charm to feeding the wonder that was felt in girlhood when seeing those decorations. It frees her to see the world as she did back then.

Marking the changing of the seasons with a change of scenery and atmosphere also provides opportunity to incorporate the cleaning routines. The mantle gets dusted and waxed when the old decorations come down and before the new season's decorations go up. The storage area is cleaned once all the Christmas bins have been brought out. The furniture is rearranged for good movement of air for summer months and the house décor is minimized so that it seems cooler.

I tend towards Victorian or a vintage flavor to my holiday celebrations. Going far to the beginning usually is a let down for me because so many of the current American holidays had a disappointing beginning in ancient times and the current celebrations are more about economy and buying than should be. It's my world and I can choose the best out of all the different eras. Not that I think that the Victorians had it all together, but I do pick and choose.

Please note that I have included the North American Christian/Jewish traditional holidays. I am not trying to leave others out or make a statement about the validity. There just wasn't room for every country and every religious content.

<u>December 31 New Years Eve</u>

There really wasn't a New Year's Eve celebration until after World War I but according to my research the Victorians had a sweet custom for New Year's Day. The young eligible men would make short calls on single young ladies. They would stop at each household and of course leave their calling cards. There were proper chaperones which often meant the whole family and light refreshments were served. It is also said that the young ladies would compete with each other as to how many cards they had collected!

So in this case, I think that some of our current celebrations are more fun. Most of us stay up and wait to greet the new year. The symbols of course are Father Time and the baby new year. Normally the colors to decorate with are blue and silver. Some traditions are to burn a bayberry candle down. Set off fireworks if it is allowed in your area. At midnight, eat 12 grapes, to bring sweetness to each month. Have a bucket of water on your front porch, and after you have eaten your 12 grapes, carry it through the house and toss it out your back door. This ushers in the new year and washes clean the past. It is the time many of us make resolutions. New Years Day brings parades that I have loved since I was a girl, especially the Rose Bowl Parade.

Some families also have special lucky foods for the new year like black-eyed peas or pork and sauerkraut. My late husband was fond of making clam chowder. Go with these ideas or start a tradition of your own.

Don't forget to kiss the man you love at the stroke of midnight.

January 6- Three Kings Day

This is the traditional day of gift giving in many Latin communities. It corresponds to the time that the three kings of the orient saw a star and followed it to the barn to present gifts to the baby Jesus. The night before the children would put out their shoes by the front door so the kings would know how many children live in the house and leave them gifts in and about the shoes. In Puerto Rico, I remember that the children also left some straw out for the camels who would be hungry after such a long travel. In Mexico a sweet yeast bread is served in the evening with a miniature doll baby and a fava bean baked into the dough. If you find the doll you will have to host the Candeleria party in February but the one who finds the bean will help you out by providing the drinks for the party.

Third Monday in January-Martin Luther King Jr Day

This is the newest of the American holidays which started in 1986. It is a day to celebrate the birth, the life and the dream of this great man. It is a time to remember the injustices that Dr. King fought along with his fight for the freedom, equality, and dignity of all races and peoples. We would decorate the mantle with Dr. King's photos and copies of his speech.

"I have a dream that one day little black boys and black girls will be able to join hands with little white boys and white girls as sisters and brothers.

I have a dream today"

February 2-Ground Hog's Day

The legend of Groundhog Day is based on an old Scottish couplet: "If Candlemas Day is bright and clear, there'll be two winters in the year."

Every February 2, people gather at Gobbler's Knob, a wooded knoll just outside of Punxsutawney, Pennsylvania.

The ceremony in Punxsutawney was held in secret until 1966, and only Phil's prediction was revealed to the public. Since then, Phil's fearless forecast has been a national media event.

The groundhog comes out of his electrically heated burrow, looks for his shadow and utters his prediction to a Groundhog Club representative in "groundhogese." The representative then translates the prediction for the general public.

If Punxsutawney Phil sees his shadow, it means six more weeks of winter. If he does not see his shadow, it means spring is just around the corner.

Approximately 90% of the time, Phil sees his shadow.

Phil started making predictions in 1887 and has become an American institution.

February 14-Valentine's Day

The legend is that the holiday became Valentine's Day after a priest named *Valentine*. Valentine was a priest in Rome at the time Christianity was a new religion. The Emperor at that time, Claudius II, ordered the Roman soldiers NOT to marry or become engaged. Claudius believed that as married men, his soldiers would want to stay home with their families rather than fight his wars. Valentine defied the Emperor's decree and secretly married the young couples. He was eventually arrested, imprisoned, and put to death

Valentine was beheaded on February 14th, the eve of the Roman holiday Lupercalia. After his death, Valentine was named a saint.

The Victorians loved to make and send Valentine cards. They made elaborate ones trimmed with satin ribbons and ornaments. They considered it bad luck to sign the card but good luck if a silver coin was placed under a young lady's pillow on Valentine's Eve because she was to receive a proposal by the end of the year. One of the more popular cards were the three dimensional fold out Valentine. These cards were first produced in Germany and England. However, with their popularity they become very prevalent in America. The cards were manufactured from pasteboard, so once they were broken they were beyond repair. The three dimensional cards are very popular with collectors today, because not many have survived over the years.

The fold-out cards were being produced from the late 1800's to the early 1900's. They were made from heavier paper board then the three dimensional cards.

The fold-out cards were covered with lace, flowers, ribbon and angels. Most of these cards were not mailed because they were large and fragile. They had to be delivered in person.

These were more than cards they were a gift. People would display them in their parlor on a table, and the card would become a topic of conversation.

In the late 1860's the album was introduced for preserving your cards. The album became all the rage. Scraps also began being produced in Germany which made the album become one of the first scrapbooks.

As you know, the Victorians loved flowers, so different types of roses became very popular on the Valentine Card. These were sometimes embossed to give the flowers realism.

The Valentine Card then started being produced with cupids, children and women. The images of the people on the cards were done to the specifications of what the Victorians believed to be beautiful. Such as; small noses, long lashes, perfect complexions, etc.

Scraps were first produced in Germany as were most of these fold out type cards. To save money the factories would produce the many scraps on a single sheet of paper to send to the wholesalers.

I love to decorate the house for Valentine's day soon after the Christmas things are put away. I took fallen branches and spray painted them white and sprinkled glitter on them while the paint was wet. From this would be lots of hearts and cupids and Valentines. I would print vintage cupids out on the computer, back them with cardboard and pose them on the mantle with other vintage valentines. I made a pretty little heart by bending wire coat hangers into shape and then wrapping narrow red lace around it. I decorated the bathroom with pink, red and white and used bulletin board border from the teachers supply store to create disposable moulding. Homemade heart soaps and other knickknacks finished the look. The weekend before, we would take doilies, construction paper and pictures printed from the computer to make home made valentines for each member of the family. Dinner was pink and red, ham, pink mashed potatoes, beets, strawberry milk and strawberry cake in a heart shape.

Third Monday of February-President's Day

When I was young, we celebrated both Lincoln and Washington's birthday. In 1971, President's Day was appointed to give a 3 day weekend and combine the two celebrations.

Americans were celebrating Washington's birthday before he had died with balls, parades, and re-enactments. And then another beloved president, Lincoln was assassinated and he also happened to have a birthday in February so both were celebrated. We liked to pull out the Lincoln logs and build Lincoln town and bake a cherry pie for the story about Washington who could not tell a lie when his father asked who chopped down the cherry tree.

The two presidents have their photos added to the mantle with little flags and some of the patriotic decorations borrowed from the fourth of July.

Day before Ash Wednesday when Lent begins-Mardi Gras

Translated from French as Fat Tuesday before the fasting begins the time of Lent. The colors for Mardi Gras are purple for justice, green for faith and gold for power. On January 1, 1830 a group of young men walking home after a New Year's eve celebration in Mobile, Alabama, passed a store featuring an outdoor display of rakes, hoes and cowbells. Being inebriated they picked up the supplies and headed to the mayor's house where they caused a commotion. He was a patient man and he sobered them up and made this group's leader an offer. Instead of getting into trouble, why not organize and let everyone have fun and that was how it has migrated into the parades and celebrations seen today. Later masks were introduced and the throwing of pretend coins and jewels. A king of the celebration was appointed and called Rex. So crowns, masks, pretend necklaces and coins in Mardi Gras colors are all a part of the festivities. There is also a special king cake that is baked with a baby doll inside. The one who gets the baby doll is responsible for making the cake the next year.

I use chocolate coins, beads of the Mardi Gras colors and masks to decorate the mantle.

14th and 15th of Adar-Purim

Purim is the most festive of Jewish holidays, a time of prizes, noisemakers, costumes and treats. The Festival of Purim commemorates a major victory over oppression and is recounted in the *Megillah*, the scroll of the story of Esther. Purim takes place on the fourteenth and fifteenth days of Adar, the twelfth month of the Jewish calendar. When the story of Megillah is read, boos, hisses, stamping of feet and noise makers are used each time Haman is mentioned. Hamantaschen are cookies baked to look like the three-cornered hat that he wore and costumes are worn.

March 17-St. Patrick's Day

This holiday began in Ireland obviously and has had interesting growth in America. It was celebrated by Irish immigrants and at one time in Europe, Queen Victoria banned the wearing of Shamrocks because it had become a symbol of rebellion. There are lots of post cards from the time that provides evidence of the acknowledgement of this holiday. Today we have parades and green foods and most of us wear green. They have a tradition of turning the Chicago river green. We have taken on the image of the leprechaun as a St. Patrick's symbol. Of course, St. Patrick was known for his preaching work in Ireland and a story about chasing out snakes. Remember on St. Patrick's day everyone is Irish!

We always would invite an Irish couple for a dinner of corned beef and cabbage. We have trouble with a leprechaun who visits our home and plays tricks. Green turns up everywhere. Even the milk magically turns green when poured in the glass that night.

I like to decorate the mantle with little green twinkle lights, shamrocks and vintage cards.

March –April- Easter

How wonderful to have pastel colors and softly warming days after a long winter! The Victorians were part of beginning of the modern Easter Bunn, first popularized in Germany in the 16th century and brought to the United States during the Victorian era. Rabbits were very popular images in Victorian Easter scrap art and cards. The first public Easter parade in America occurred in 1860 in Atlantic City, New Jersey, when families strolled along the Boardwalk in their new Spring finery from the command of Constantine in the third century to wear our best clothes. Don't forget your Easter bonnet. We always had a table with a little Easter village and of course we had it all sitting on Easter grass. That pesky Easter bunny kept sneaking into the house and bringing in candy right up until Easter eve. That's when we color eggs and that wily rabbit would steal them and hide them on us. We knew it was him because there was suspicious white paw prints on the carpet and Easter grass in the door. We forgave him when we found all the beautiful Easter clothes he left behind.

I bring out the 'tree" from Valentine's day and it is used for the egg shells we have decorated by blowing out the eggs from a pin hole and then hand painting the egg shells. Little pastel bows are added and twinkle lights.

The mantle is decorated with ceramic bunnies, chocolate foil eggs and vintage cards printed out.

March-April- Passover

Passover runs for 8 days and reminds us of the freedom and exodus of the Israelites from Egypt during the reign of Pharaoh Ramses II. Families get together and have lavish meals called Seders. The story of Passover is told and remembered with special foods, songs and customs.

Second Sunday in May- Mother's Day

In England, many of the poor had a long way to go to work at the home of their employer and so most of them would live in the home in which they served. On mothering Sunday they were encouraged to go home and visit their mothers and take them small gifts and cakes. In the United States, the idea of a Mother's day was first suggested by Julia Ward Howe who had written the words to the Battle Hymn of the Republic. She organized Mother's day meetings in Boston but it really caught on in 1907 when Ana Jarvis from Philadelphia began a campaign to establish a national holiday, suggesting the day of her own mother's death.

My favorite Mother's day was when my youngest son took us out to breakfast at the restaurant he was working at then. After our delicious breakfast, he had someone bring out a dozen roses from the fridge. The whole restaurant applauded and I cried big tears.

Third Sunday in June-Father's Day

About the same time as the idea for Mother's day was growing in popularity, the birth of Father's day was also being considered. It wasn't a national holiday until 1966 which explains why I don't remember it as much as a child. It also might be that it is a holiday that happens when school is out and so we were not as focused on it.

David, used to call Father's day, weird tie day because the children and I always picked out a wild tie and shirt to match. He was a good sport and wore them to church anyway.

Serve up his favorite dinner. He deserves it after the ugly tie business.

Early Summer- Shavuot

The Feast of the Weeks which is a celebration of the harvest season corresponding to this happening 7 weeks after Passover. It is also known as the Day of the First Fruits when farmers would take their first fruits to Jerusalem as their thanksgiving gift. It is also the commemoration of the anniversary of the giving of the Ten Commandments to Moses. It is a time of holding vigil and eating of dairy foods like blintz and cheesecake.

Homes and synagogues are often decorated with branches and flowers as well.

July 4th-Independence Day

The birthday celebration of the United States. Picnics and fireworks shows mark this event. There were also many vintage cards commemorating this event. A surprising number included children setting off fireworks!

This is normally our first picnic of the year. We decorate with red, white and blue of course. Flags are flown and then we head out for fireworks bringing blankets popcorn popped the old way and placed in a brown paper bag and lemonade.

Did you know that there is flag etiquette? The flag is to be flown only from sunrise to sunset unless there is a light on it. It should never touch the ground. If it is placed at a podium, it should always be to the right of the speaker. If it is flown with a state, city or community flag, the US flag should always be at the top. If it is flown half-staff for mourning, it should first be hoisted to the top and then placed at half staff. When it is taken down, it should again be hoisted to the top and then lowered. The stars are to be flown near the pole.

Early Autumn-High Holy Days

"The Jewish High Holy Days are observed during the 10 day period between the first day (Rosh Hashanah) and the 10th day (Yom Kippur) of Tishri, the seventh month of the Jewish calendar.

Rosh Hashanah and Yom Kippur are the most important of all Jewish Holidays and the only holidays that are purely religious, as they are not related to any historical or natural event.

Rosh Hashanah, the Jewish New Year, is celebrated the first and second days of Tishri. It is a time of family gatherings, special meals and sweet tasting foods.

Yom Kippur, the Day of Atonement, is the most solemn day of the Jewish year and is observed on the tenth day of Tishri. It is a day of fasting, reflection and prayers." –from Holidays on the Net

Last Monday in September- Labor Day

Back in 1894, Congress passed an act making this a legal holiday. The central Labor Union wanted a street parade followed by a festival for the recreation and amusement of workers and their families. Speeches by prominent persons came later and it now seen as an outdoor gathering and end of summer barbeque by people today.

I had a very memorable Labor day. I was in labor for my firstborn back in 1980. It worked out nicely because his father had the day off anyway! We use Labor day as the last picnic of the season. I normally rearrange the furniture to make better use of the heating vents. I do a good cleaning to get ready for the busy holiday season ahead. We normally finish the garden work by then. The decorations from the fourth of July are taken down from the mantle after labor day. And then we begin with the scarecrows and harvest décor.

October 31- Halloween

It seems lately that there has been an attempt to change this into harvest festivals because of the evil connotations. I have my own personal opinion on this which I am glad to share. I think that dressing up and pretending we are someone else fills a child's imagination no matter how old she may be. (Yes, I do dress for Halloween). As for having it's background in Non-Christian traditions…that is true of so many things that we accept as ours, that it doesn't make a difference to me either. I love the way they celebrated back at the turn of the century and prefer that vintage/Victorian mystery and childlikeness. There is quite a bit of clip art with pumpkins, little girls dressed as witches, black cats and owls and bats. The Halloween parties then involved play acting, costumes and whimsical fortune telling. Bobbing for apples and lots of treats were also a part of it. Some of the Irish immigrants enjoyed playing pranks like tipping over outhouses. The recounting of ghost stories around the fire were also a part of the fun.

I am not into scaring little children but I do love the stretching of imagination and jack-o-lanterns and orange and black and purple of the season. Whatever it's background, the celebrating I do is innocent and fun. The house is decorated with pumpkins and autumn colored leaves.

Fourth Thursday in November- Thanksgiving

I suppose that everyone reading this knows that Thanksgiving had to do with the meal shared by the pilgrims and Indians, thanking God for a bountiful harvest. It became a national holiday by declaration of Abraham Lincoln.

I decorate by adding to the autumn décor up since September. Horn of plenty baskets are used and turkeys and little pilgrim/Indian figures. This is the time the family gets together for a big turkey feast and shares what blessings have been bestowed during the year. The next day, is our day to begin putting up the Christmas decorations especially the tree. We have ulterior motives for this. Some of the grown children are usually here to help with the tasks!

Early December- Chanukah

Chanukah, the Festival of Lights, is a celebration of the victory of the Maccabees and the rededication of the Jerusalem Temple. It also commemorates the miracle of the oil that burned for 8 days. Part of this holiday involves the menorah, spinning the dreidel.

December 25- Christmas

The traditional remembrance of the birth of the Christ child. The thinking is that Martin Luther decorated a small tree with candles to tell the story and soon trees were being decorated all across Germany. Real silver was made into strands of tinsel and hung with the candles. Then Queen Victoria made Christmas trees even more fashionable and many young ladies were creating ornaments from quilled paper, beads and baskets. Germany began to produce beautiful ornaments and lately for safety sakes, we have given up the candles for lights. Other religious symbols are candy canes and stockings.

Then there is the jolly old elf. Santa Claus has many different stories associated with him according to the country celebrating. In the US we have the story about him and the 8 tiny reindeer who pull his sled based on the story *The Night before Christmas* by Clement Moore. Our Christmas is partly based on that and the Charles Dickens story about Scrooge. I think with the coming of TV and video, we have also added more to the ideas. I was definitely affected by watching Rudolf the red-nosed reindeer as a child. I have to think that the Santa Clause movies and the train movie have captured more of our children's imagination.

I love Christmas. I love the secular and the religious aspects but as an adult, I am able to separate the two easily enough. Make sure your children know the story of Christ and please consider taking them to a Christmas eve service, especially if it is a candlelit service. There is nothing so fulfilling to me. It was a great honor to sing in the choir during these services and a couple of times sing a solo of "Oh Holy Night". So full of meaning and so full of awe to see a service like this.

The secondary part of Christmas is the glittering feeding of imaginations in children. I don't care how old, Santa is real in our house. We throw carrots up on the roof and find some of them half eaten with hoof prints in the snow. (and how did that goat get loose last night?) Santa loves the cookies and hot cocoa we leave for him and he always leaves a letter thanking the children for being good and encouraging them on goals to work on next year. I do wish he would learn to wipe his feet though. I always have to clean sparkly snow dust from the carpet. What whoops and hollers are filling the air Christmas morning when little ones find all the presents he left behind for them!

As for decorating, I don't have to tell you do I? Our house looks like a winter wonderland. We have two trees. One is the fancy glass bobbles and big lights and tinsel that I remember from my childhood. The other is one that is so busy it can make one dizzy. All the crazy moving ornaments, the ones the children made over the years, the lights that are planned to move according to the music they play, and red bubble lights, too.

The main bathroom is decorated with snowmen. There is a sleigh being pulled by three tiny flamingos. I am living in Florida after all and Fairman is a crazy man. Rudolf looks on in disbelief.

There is a wreath on the front door, and candles in every window. There are angels on the mantle and lights on anything that looks like it might be a tree. Poinsettias grace the patio. Christmas cards are suspended from ribbons along the wall. It is beautiful and not too gaudy, yet. This takes about a week which brings us to about the first of December. I get my shopping done by Halloween if possible but no later than Thanksgiving, wrapping as I go along. Next, I concentrate on secondary gifts. Consumables are the best thing to give that won't eventually add to the land fill problem. Nut mixes and home made cookies. I like to bake a different kind every morning but some years just are not as organized as I hope. Those are the years I go for marathon baking. One big mess and one big clean up but it brings out dozens of presents with trays of cookies wrapped in pretty colored food wrap and tied up with ribbon. This gets mailed to far away relatives, given to the mail lady, yard man, paper girl, teachers, co-workers and neighbors.

On Christmas eve all children regardless of age, open stockings, drink cocoa and eat cookies and we sing carols. If there are little ones, a Christmas story is read. Christmas morning, is spent with a nice breakfast and finally we open presents. Santa left his hat one year and told us we could keep it so we use it as a tradition. The person wearing the hat opens his present and then finds one for someone else and places the hat on their head and the present on their lap. Later we have a big Christmas dinner and a bit of wine around the fire. More carols are sung and sometimes, little skits. I just love Christmas.

There are also the birthdays to celebrate with cake and candles and wishes and presents. And anniversary cakes, too. UF women look for other things to celebrate as well. Promotions, new babies, bon voyage parties, lots of fun things.

Live life well by recognizing special days. Organize the passing of time with celebrations. Dressing up, special foods and music, traditions, and lots of fun keep the child-like spirit alive in all of us.

Chapter 7
She is Charitable

Everything that I am going to suggest to you is a benefit to you, your self-esteem, your soul. Please keep this close to your heart as you read on.

Did you read the book or see the movie "Pay it Forward"? It is about a boy whose philosophy of life is that the world would be a better place if everyone tried to "pay it forward" by helping a stranger, and by that stranger in turn helping another. How great is that? Can you think of a time that someone, maybe someone you didn't know offered you a hand when you needed it? Pay it forward.

Do you know about the Random Acts of Kindness movement? They have one hundred suggestions on RAK's web site and have offered them to any and all:

100 IDEAS FOR KINDNESS

1. Deliver fresh-baked cookies to city workers.
2. Collect goods for a food bank.
3. Bring flowers to work and share them with coworkers.
4. Garden clubs can make floral arrangements for senior centers, nursing homes, hospitals, police stations, or shut-ins.
5. Adopt a student who needs a friend, checking in periodically to see how things are going.
6. Volunteer to be a tutor in a school.
7. Extend a hand to someone in need. Give your full attention and simply listen.
8. Merchants can donate a percentage of receipts for the week to a special cause.
9. Bring coworkers a special treat.
10. Students can clean classrooms for the custodian.
11. Buy a stranger a free pizza.
12. Distribute lollipops to kids.
13. Sing at a nursing home.
14. Offer a couple of hours of baby-sitting to parents.
15. Slip paper hearts that say "It's Random Acts of Kindness Week! Have a great day!" under the windshield wipers of parked cars.
16. Have a charity day at work, with employees bringing nonperishable food items to donate.
17. Serve refreshments to customers.
18. Draw names at school or work, and have people bring a small gift or food treat for their secret pal.
19. Remember the bereaved with phone calls, cards, plants, and food.
20. Treat someone to fresh fruit.
21. Pay a compliment at least once a day.
22. Call or visit a homebound person.
23. Hand out balloons to passersby.
24. Give free sodas to motorists.
25. Be a good neighbor. Take over a baked treat or stop by to say "Hello."
26. Transport someone who can't drive.
27. Mow a neighbor's grass.
28. Say something nice to everyone you meet today.
29. Send a treat to a school or day-care center.
30. Volunteer at an agency that needs help.
31. Wipe rainwater off shopping carts or hold umbrellas for shoppers on the way to their cars.
32. Give the gift of your smile.
33. Send home a note telling parents something their child did well.
34. Adopt a homeless pet at the humane society.
35. Organize a scout troop or service club to help people with packages at the mall or grocery.

36. Host special programs or speakers at libraries or bookstores.
37. Offer to answer the phone for the school secretary for ten minutes.
38. Volunteer to read to students in the classroom.
39. Write notes of appreciation and bring flowers or goodies to teachers or other important people, such as the principal, nurse, custodian, and secretary.
40. Incorporate kindness into the curriculum at area schools, day care centers, or children's classes in faith organizations.
41. Give a hug to a friend.
42. Tell your children why you love them.
43. Write a note to your mother/father and tell them why they are special.
44. Pat someone on the back.
45. Write a thank-you note to a mentor or someone who has influenced your life in a positive way.
46. Give coffee to people on their way to work in the morning.
47. Donate time at a senior center.
48. Give blood.
49. Visit hospitals with smiles, treats, and friendly conversation for patients.
50. Stop by a nursing home, and visit a resident with no family nearby.
51. Plant flowers in your neighbor's flower box.
52. Give another driver your parking spot.
53. Leave a treat or handmade note of thanks for a delivery person or mail carrier.
54. Give free car washes.
55. Clean graffiti from neighborhood walls and buildings.
56. Tell your boss that you think he/she does a good job.
57. Tell your employees how much you appreciate their work.
58. Let your staff leave work an hour early.
59. Have a clean-up party in the park.
60. Tell a bus or taxi driver how much you appreciate their driving.
61. Have everyone in your office draw the name of a Random Acts of Kindness buddy out of a hat and do a kind act for their buddy that day or week.
62. Give a pair of tickets to a baseball game or concert to a stranger.
63. Leave an extra big tip for the waitperson.
64. Drop off a plant, cookies, or donuts to the police or fire department.
65. Open the door for another person.
66. Pay for the meal of the person behind you in the drive-through.
67. Write a note to the boss of someone who has helped you, praising the employee.
68. Leave a bouquet of flowers on the desk of a colleague at work with whom you don't normally get along.
69. Call an estranged family member.
70. Volunteer to fix up an elderly couple's home.
71. Pay for the person behind you in the movie line.
72. Give flowers to be delivered with meal delivery programs.
73. Give toys to the children at the shelter or safe house.
74. Give friends and family kindness coupons they can redeem for kind favors.
75. Be a friend to a new student or coworker.
76. Renew an old friendship by sending a letter or small gift to someone you haven't talked with in a long time.
77. For one week, act on every single thought of generosity that arises spontaneously in your heart, and notice what happens as a consequence.
78. Offer to return a shopping cart to the store for someone loading a car.
79. Invite someone new over for dinner.
80. Buy a roll of brightly colored stickers and give them to children you meet during the day.
81. Write a card of thanks and leave it with your tip. Be sure to be specific in your thanks.
82. Let the person behind you in the grocery store go ahead of you in line.
83. When drivers try to merge into your lane, let them in with a wave and a smile.
84. Buy cold drinks for the people next to you at a ball game.
85. Distribute kindness bookmarks that you have made.
86. Create a craft project or build a bird house with a child.
87. Give a bag of groceries to a homeless person.
88. Laugh out loud often and share your smile generously.
89. Plant a tree in your neighborhood.
90. Make a list of things to do to bring more kindness into the world, and have a friend make a list. Exchange lists and do one item per day for a month.

91. Use an instant camera to take people's photographs at a party or community event, and give the picture to them.
92. As you go about your day, pick up trash.
93. Send a letter to some former teachers, letting them know the difference they made in your life.
94. Send a gift anonymously to a friend.
95. Organize a clothing drive for a shelter.
96. Buy books for a day care or school.
97. Slip a $20 bill to a person who you know is having financial difficulty.
98. Take an acquaintance to dinner.
99. Offer to take a friend's child to ball practice.
100. Waive late fees for the week.

Do you find it easy to slip a dollar into a tip jar or even the kettle for the Salvation Army but don't feel comfortable finding ways to offer charity yourself? Many of us are like that. I have always felt better when I knew what I was offering was really needed. So I like assignments. I thought I would share some of the times I was able to share my time with organizations and what I received out of that.

I was a volunteer leader for La Leche League years ago. That was very fulfilling work, helping new mothers with breastfeeding and organizing meetings. I found a niche in a night group for mothers who worked. They deserved a lot of credit in trying to give their babies the best that they could while holding to an outside job. I did what I could to support and encourage them. This was a very fulfilling time in my life. It brought with it a position of prestige in the hospital because I was called in by doctors, nurses or friends of new moms needing help. I had to step down when there were complications with my last baby and I no longer had the time to devote.

After my children were raised, I volunteered for several years with Hospice. That was such a wonderful thing for me. I was probably the last friend that my patients made on this earth and it was an honor to be that friend in their last days. My patients all had "good deaths", meaning that they lived to the end with dignity and pain management. It was very spiritual to be at their side in this journey. It was just such an honor.

I loved volunteering for projects at church as well, especially singing in the choir. It was also a good place to make secret gifts where it was especially needed. I love making secret donations. It feels right to me. When I hear about a young family just trying to get by, I could leave a bit of money in the envelope in the plate, with the request to please see to the young family and our priest always saw to it. Sometimes, we would make a special donation to the nursery and love to see the new books, games and decorations.

I hate to suggest that foster care was charitable, because it was just so much fun to have the kids in our home and it didn't cost anything. That is the best sort of giving, the kind that feeds your heart so much that you don't see it as a sacrifice. It can be fun to volunteer. The world is full of martyrs but God loves a cheerful giver. Find something that you love and donate to it. If money is in short supply in your budget, then volunteer your talents, or even just your time.

Ultimate Femininity has a pet charity that we work with. "The Red Thread" is an organization that works to get orphans needed surgery, help with hard-hit areas and those less fortunate. As a community, we make things for others and receive a sense of fulfillment from knowing we are making a difference. We have a UF group called "The Gifts of her Hands" and we make goals and efforts to help others in this way.

So why is being charitable a feminine quality? Throughout history women have been the sensitive creatures who notice the small things that may pass by their husband unnoticed. A woman will organize with her sisters to make things better, to bring comfort and to assist quietly as it is almost an urge within her to protect those who cannot protect themselves. She may shudder at violence and stand behind her husband in fear of a stranger at the door but let someone threaten harm to her children and she becomes a mother bear who will back anyone down. This protective nature also comes out if someone smaller or weaker is threatened. Remember Dorothy from the "Wizard of Oz" when the lion threatened her little dog? She stood up firm against the would-be beast and slapped him on the face. UF women are like that, they are strong when the need comes for them to be and it is this quality that fulfills us when we are able to come to the rescue of another.

We live in a time that a few have much and many have little. Although we can't save the world, we can make a difference. I realized that when I took in children, that I would be sending them home and always, the home they would return to made our house seem like a castle. It gradually dawned on me that I was only taking children out of low living conditions for a year or so but that I could not save them from a childhood of poverty or teen pregnancy or single parenting later on. The only thing I could do is give them a taste of normal for a small time and hopefully when they came of age, they would work towards higher goals. Maybe, I hope, that the small time they spent with us, made a difference.

So making a blanket to comfort a child for a while seems like a very small thing but it may be that child's first real possession. It might mean that a gift from a far-away stranger gives that child hope and strength to fight through surgery and be more healthy. It could be the thing that makes a difference but more than that, it will fulfill you. The reason that there is more happiness in giving is because it fills the soul, it makes us think of someone else instead of our own miserable problems.

There will be more about this in the last chapter but there was a time in my life when I was sorely depressed. And somehow it occurred to me to go help some of the older ones in our congregation. The kids and I made cookies and we delivered them to the shut-ins that we knew. We made lists of the things they needed, groceries, clothing, house and yard work and we scheduled them into our Sunday routines. We took cookies to those in nursing homes and visited some of the sick in the hospital. The children loved it and it was a magic elixir for my mental stability. I looked forward to each day again and I learned a valuable lesson. Help others and stop moping! Choose happiness.

My daughter learned at my side. She was a "big sister" and a spokesperson for that organization in her community. She loved spending time with her "little sister" and has lots of pictures of this little girl growing into a beautiful young lady. My sons always go out of their way to help older folks, taking out the trash for them or mowing the yard.

You really don't have to go through an organization if you don't want to. You will see a need and answer it when you begin to look at life in that way. This is something you are doing for you. This is your life road, traveled once and yet, you touch millions.

Sometimes people are afraid to stick their nose in if it isn't wanted. And yes, sometimes it is hard to know when it is ok and not ok to offer a hand. For example, there are some street people who make a living from being street people and there are those who don't. How do you know which one is which? You don't want to help a person stay in a lifestyle that is unhealthy. There was a documentary about how a homeless man dealt with 100,000 dollars that was given to him. He went through it quickly and is back on the streets. The root problems often have to do with drug and alcohol abuse, mental illness and lack of family support, all things that are not easily fixed but, can you hand a homeless person something to eat? If there is someone asking for money on your regular routes, I have a suggestion. Put together individual sized pull tab type cans of food, like fruit, Vienna sausages, tuna, or a bag from a fast food place. Let them know that you can't give them money but here is a bite to eat, or a cup of coffee if it is cold out. If this is difficult to consider, then use a go-between. Find out where there is a food pantry in your community and ask them what is needed. Please resist the idea to get rid of old unwanted food from your kitchen because outdated food is normally thrown out. Keep in mind that with a few bad decisions or bad luck, it could have been you. Count your blessings but try not to judge those less fortunate.

I hope that something said in this chapter has piqued your interest and will allow you to feel warmth and fulfillment that opening your hand to give to others, can bring.

Chapter 8
She is Happy

<u>Choosing to be happy</u>
My fiancé Fairman sent this to me one morning. His sister sent it to him and he thought of me. I have been through some difficult things in life, but, I have tried very hard to remember that I could choose to be happy. It is, after all, what my late husband wanted. Here is the little story my beloved sent to me:

There once was a woman who woke up one morning, looked in the mirror, and noticed she had only three hairs on her head. "Well," she said, "I think I'll braid my hair today."? So she did and she had a wonderful day.

The next day she woke up, looked in the mirror and saw that she had only two hairs on her head. "H-M-M, " she said, "I think I'll part my hair down the middle today." So she did and she had a grand day.

The next day she woke up, looked in the mirror and noticed that she had only one hair on her head. "Well," she said, "Today I'm going to wear my hair in a pony tail." So she did and she had a fun, fun day.

The next day she woke up, looked in the mirror and noticed that there wasn't a single hair on her head. "YEAH!" she exclaimed, "I don't have to fix my hair today!"

Attitude is everything. As the saying goes: "The kind of life you will have isn't determined by what happens to you, it's determined by your reaction to what happens to you."

Be kind, for everyone you meet is fighting some kind of battle.

_____author unknown_____

It would be so easy to give into the depths of despair. In my younger days I did. I didn't know how to be a young wife and mother. I didn't know how to find pleasure and happiness in that role even though it was my choice to be there. I kept thinking, "what is wrong with me?" Nothing was wrong with me except my attitude. I went searching for all that was wrong with my life instead of focusing on all that was right. I didn't know how to fill my glass so that it was overflowing enough to give to the important people in my life.

Please understand that you need to accept mourning and loss as part of your life. When you have loss, you absolutely must accept the necessity to mourn that loss, to embrace the pain that goes with it. Being afraid of the pain, may keep you mourning for a much longer time. I spent a week alone in the darkest pits of Hades. The pain I felt on the loss of my husband was excruciating, there is nothing I can compare it to. It was physically taxing, it was hard work to come out of it alive. It was the hardest thing I have ever done, to let him go. I did all the things I thought I should. If someone asked me to go somewhere, I went but I could not concentrate enough on the conversations to follow them well. I was lost in my sorrow and kept thinking how could life possibly still be going on around me? I found the man I loved dead, gone to me forever, how could it be real? It didn't seem to me that the world should still be spinning, that meals should be prepared, that I should get up out of the bed we shared, that I should lie down in it or that I should even breathe at times. Other times, the anger enveloped me like a big black cloud that just took me up in a funnel and exploded in anguish and more anger than I have ever known. I would go out where I found him and scream at him for having left me alone.

This is how it is in life. All of you have things that you must mourn. I hope it is never as severe as what I faced but even the little things that cause changes in your life must be mourned and accepted. If you will do this, in healthy ways, you can see how to choose to be happy. It is a choice. Unless you have clinical depression (and if so, please, please get medical intervention) living sad is also a choice.

When you choose "happy", you will see life differently than the rest of the world. You will look for beauty in nature. A beautiful flower, a sunset, a deer in a meadow will thrill you. You will look for the beauty in others even when they have trouble finding it. After all, life is very short and you only have a limited time to make a difference in the world. Could a positive compliment have changed the course of someone's life if you had only offered it? Maybe just a smile, or human touch?

LIFE IS NOT MEASURED BY THE NUMBER OF BREATHS WE TAKE, BUT BY THE MOMENTS THAT TAKE OUR BREATH AWAY.--author unknown

This is another one that Fairman sent to me and it is just so true. Many people work hard for a better car, a better home, nicer furniture, the latest fashions, the best toys for their children and so on it goes.

I have known poverty. I remember times when the TV broke or we couldn't afford cable which amounted to be the same. We read more. We sat on a blanket in the yard and watched for shooting stars. We listened to the radio. We played cards and games. We had conversations. We watched the sun come up or watched it go down. Those were special times. Really, do you think your children will look back and remember all those wonderful evenings sitting around the TV set? I am not saying there is anything wrong with having a TV (yikes shall I count up how many we have...1, 2, 3, 4) but the little things are really what life is all about. I do have a suggestion. What about a night at the movies, with popcorn and treats? Spread a blanket on the floor and pillows about, turn down the lights and pretend you are in a theater. I remember this as a child watching The Wonderful World of Disney on Sunday nights. When my kids were little we would rent Videos for our movie night.

For me, times that take breath away are related to nature, picnics, road trips, time at the sea shore, nature hikes, watching the antics of the birds or wild animals. We just got back from a road trip to Missouri. The trees were just changing and it was a wonder to us. We miss such things living in Florida....the butterflies migrating, geese in V-formation... the smell of the autumn in a cool breeze.

Did you ever create a winter picnic? After the first snow, we would bundle the kids up and head for the park with sleds. The picnic was a thermos of hot tomato soup with a hot dog with a string attached. They could pull out the hot dog and put it in a bun and drink the soup. Of course they thought I was crazy but they still loved it, but more, they remember it still as grown-ups out on their own.

Have you explored the nature parks in your area? I have never been disappointed by any of them I have been to. There seems to always be a surprise within. A pretty bridge over a creek, or a waterfall or wild flowers in bloom. Go exploring with your family.

Those of you who have new babies have many, many moments that take your breath away. Write every night about the special firsts. See the special discoveries your little one makes through his eyes. I remember how excited one of mine was when he first really took notice of water. It just ran through his little fingers as he tried to grab it. He had the most amazed look as he tried and tried to pick it up. This is a wonderful thing for grandmas to do also.

Gardening also allows for breath-taking moments. When you tend to young plants and they bloom or give fruit, it is so fulfilling. A small thing to tend a young rose but it seems so much when you first discover that little bud and later the bloom. Watching those yellow blooms on tomatoes and then they fruit and turn red. It gives you reason to go outdoors every morning just to see what is new.

Are you worth it? That often times seems to be the question. Women are such tending creatures that they feel they must take care of everyone. Everyone depends on them. Emotional needs from so many takes a great deal from the women in the world. Sometimes it is just not the family. Sometimes, it is parents or siblings or friends who need them just so much. And so these women of tender mercy decide that it is just some time to listen, just some ears to hear and not once do they take into account that each time they give emotionally or physically to another person, a part of their own self is shared.

Think back to a time when you were a support for another human. Do you remember being very tired? Did you feel some of your own strength go out from you? Those of you who are Christians might understand this in a spiritual way. It is a bit of Holy Spirit that you are sharing almost like electricity flows. Remember how Christ knew that someone had touched him? The woman with the flow of blood received some of the Spirit and was healed and Jesus felt the motion.

Understand that you give and it is a spiritual thing no matter what your faith is but that you must also take in. A wise woman knows that her husband deserves a refreshed, lively woman who has a zest for life and always seems to be so giving. The secret to being such a woman is knowing what will fill your glass. What makes you happy? What makes you feel that zest for life?

How do you know it is important to see to those needs? You will begin to feel resentment. That is actually a hunger and need not be negative. You need to see to your emotional needs and see it as an unselfish thing that will make you better equipped to be there for others who need you. Holy ones often went into nature alone to refresh themselves. That was seen as a good and positive thing. Why wouldn't you also need such refreshment? Recreation means that you re-create yourself. This is a good positive and healthy thing. Don't let anything, or anyone make you feel otherwise. How can you be who you need to be without it?

There are some who will tell you that you are self-centered (though the only ones who normally say such things are we...ourselves who think we must play the martyr) and if someone does think so, you just tell them that you are a princess and worth it! Said with a smile, this takes care of most negativity.

Depression steals our strength. UF has been teaching for several years now that women are not weaklings. We choose to allow our husbands to be leaders in our home but we often are the heart and strength and binding in that home. We are the ones to keep our families in love for as long as we are alive. We are the center of the home and how we are, is reflected in our home.

Have you been to the home of a woman who is clinically depressed but she has not sought help? I know many who were like that and their homes reflected it. It was almost as if a dark cloud had descended down into the rooms and crept like swirls of smoke about the family members. I have seen women in deep depression and they hid away into darkness. The curtains closed tight on the world. It was not a home of laughter it was more a tomb for the living. It hurt to be there. So, I take them by the hand and lead them out. The sunshine, the air, creation all are a beginning to living again. Walking, getting the heart pumping, feeling warmth rush in to all body parts.

When at last we come back home, I ask them to call someone to help and that I won't leave until they do. If they try to argue, I tell them that I will need a blanket and pillow. No arguments. I won't leave. If they really don't need help, the professional will tell them so. Please understand that we all have limits and unless you have a degree behind your name, you can't treat anyone else. All you can do is urge them to get the professional help they need.

Someone who is slightly depressed can sometimes do some things for herself. Talking to someone she trusts, or typing like we do, may be a good healing thing to do. I have quite a number of friends who must call me when something new happens. I cry and laugh with them and I understand that they need me for this. What an honor to be there for them. There are some who will understand that stress needs to be placed in order. They need to make an appointment with themselves once a week to write about it and stress for one hour. The rest of the week, they have to put off worrying.

Some people need to find ways to help themselves by helping others. Feeling needed is a good thing for the soul. That is one of the mainstays in UF. Giving to others. Something to lose our sorrows in. Something bigger than ourselves.

Then we have our prayers. Ask for others to pray for you. Trust in God. Don't give it all out to HIM and then grab it back. Throw it all out there. He made us. He can handle it.

If an arm is broken. Get it in a cast. If your spirit is broken, get the pills. I would have been dead a few centuries ago because they didn't have c-sections. I gave birth to a 10 lb 3 oz child. I am thankful for the benefits of medical advances. If you need it, it takes a strong woman to admit it and go get help and take the medication. A weak one stays in her pain.

And UF leaders aren't just here supporting women who choose to stay home. Many women feel the need to work outside the home and we embrace them as sisters. Not a single one of us know another's circumstance and my feeling is that all of you are such women of character that if you are working outside the home it is for good reason. Our statement at the bottom of the welcome page on the website really sums it up well....

"We believe that a woman can find deep fulfillment from listening to her heart, and caring for her home and family. If time and resources allow, she may also open her hand to the world through church involvement, charitable service, or anonymous contributions. We offer our support to all women who put their families first, including those whose circumstances necessitate working away from home."

With that said, we also give a lot of commendation to women who choose to work at home. It has become unfashionable. It has become so out of the norm that women who choose to do so are looked down upon. Ultimate Femininity is about giving strength and worth to the role of women. And because these women work at home they have special issues to deal with. Many have tried to stay home and find that the major downside is loneliness and solitude. Or perhaps they came to that feeling when they were on maternity leave. The shift from being in an active work environment to being in the presence of only a child has been known to lead to depression from isolation. So here we are. Encouraging women to find self-worth in their role. Giving them suggestions to do more for the world in the way of charity and social work. And strengthening her role as homemaker by encouraging her to go the second mile. To learn crafts and talents that are nearly lost. Teaching women no matter what economic role they play in the family to become secure in their gender. We teach them how to find validation at home while many in the workplace fear they will find none.

Some feel that they will throw away their education or their promising growth in a career by being home. Tell me one job that is more important than raising children to become independent people of stature who will make a difference in the world. Tell me, please if it isn't possible to support a man emotionally, concentrating on his needs so that his career benefits the family fully in opposition to two mediocre careers because emotional care is lacking for both husband and wife, not to mention what this does to the marriage.

All of us make choices, but when I am laid in my grave, will my mark on the world be that I was a top executive or that I was a beloved mother and wife and friend to many. Since the latter is my goal, I work towards it. I know that my tombstone will not read "here lies CEO for AT&T". But if I chance affecting the outcome of my true goal in life by changing the dynamics in our family is it really worth the risk? Neither am I saying here that a CEO for AT&T can't be a wonderful mother, wife, friend. It all depends on where the main focus is by each woman. We all make decisions. We also must make sure that those decisions have the impact that we desire them to have.

Most of the time, it is cheaper for mom to stay home. That doesn't seem fair but we all have seen the numbers. Daycare, transportation, food, clothing and such add up and then it gets really scary when you think about the way that a woman at home cuts expenses in home cooking, errands, emotional support, etc.

There are some real benefits to being home though especially for moms. No troubles balancing childcare especially when a kid is sick. And no worries about safety of children in childcare or with a nanny. There is more time to juggle responsibilities and errands and more focus can go on the children.

So to conclude let me just say that the lifestyle that we hold dear at UF is pretty much what everyone sees as important. That women grow in their self-worth and strengths and that they be happy in their role of life. I think that you will find it attracts working women and those who work at home.

I also want to encourage women to have a small income of their own from skills that they have mastered and hopefully not having to lose the peaceful calm of their homes. How nice to be able to sell things they have made or services they have learned from home.

Hope this clarifies our stand. And I hope that all of your spirits are choosing to be happy because it is a matter of having self-worth. There she goes. A woman who carries her chin high, wearing a lacey pink dress and a matching scarf that flows as she walks. She wears modest heels, hair that obviously is seen by professionals every couple of months, natural looking make-up. She is striking not so much in her beauty but by standing out as so feminine and so self assured. She smiles at people and yes...there it was...two men nearly fought with each other to open the door for her.

There goes another one. She is of the plain community according to her appearance but she too is beautiful from an inside glow. She too, is warming the hearts of all people about her with that same self-assured smile.

And there is one more! She too carries herself well, dressed in a simple cotton blouse with lace about the color and a denim jumper. With her are two beautiful little children. The daughter is obviously being well brought up because already you can see the purposeful walk of the little girl as she charms all in the vicinity wearing a little red polka-dot dress full of ruffles and there is her brother...already a gentleman offering to carry groceries for mother and holding the door for his sister and several other passers-by. He too, is dressed neatly and there is something special about him. He seems to cherish the women in his life and bask in their appreciation of him.

These women are all different from different walks of life but they have that certain something special. They know how to self-nurture, they know that if their glass gets low, they have no more to spill out on those they love so they keep up with doing the things they love, knowing that in actuality it is an act of love for others and not about self-love. They indulge in candlelit bubble baths on hectic days and a little piece of dark chocolate which is savored daily. Some of them paint, some have tea ceremonies, some get their nails done, some have sushi and Champaign on Sunday night. All of them are secure in the role...all of them are happy being women.

These UF women are well-read, keeping up with the UF book club. They are up with current events. They hold their own in conversations. Their husbands are proud to have them on arm at parties, social gatherings and at functions from work. More than one husband has credited his wife for his attainment of promotions within the company he works.

These women are involved in volunteerism. You can find them at the school when they have children...always the first to volunteer time and services. The older UF woman has time to devote more to the community at large and she may have several pet projects that she is involved in. Even those with pre-school children work quietly at home making blankets and other things for The Red Thread or other organizations according to her time and finances.

And that home is tidy and warm and like a little enchanted cottage even when in actuality, it is an apartment on the East side of town. She uses the homemaking class and support group to organize her cleaning routines and to constantly learn new ways of displaying her femininity in her home. She is never alone. Her home may shine out but she is running the same routines as women all over the world.

She has so many friends. They flock about her, recognizing that something special that she has but never quite knowing what that something is. They hope that they can be like her. They want to know her secret for always being so happy. They would never understand that she is happy because she chooses to be!

And when that UF woman puts her head to the pillow at night, she whispers prayers of gratitude that she was created woman and was given the ability to make the world better in her own quiet ways every single day. That is her secret self-confidence. She loves being a woman.

www.ingramcontent.com/pod-product-compliance
Lightning Source LLC
LaVergne TN
LVHW091202080426
835509LV00006B/799